Vol. 10　　　　　Queer Milton　　　　　2014

Published by Clemson University Press
801 Strode Tower
Clemson, SC 29634

© 2019 Clemson University

ISBN 978-1-949979-10-7

ISSN: 1939-0246

Contents

Queer Milton
Issue Editors: Will Stockton and Daniel L. Orvis

An Introduction Justifying Queer Ways   1
    Will Stockton

"Fellowships of Joy": Angelic Union in *Paradise Lost*   14
    Stephen Guy-Bray

Eros and Anteros: Queer Mutuality in   24
Milton's *Doctrine and Discipline of Divorce*
    David L. Orvis

"What Hath Night to Do with Sleep?": Biopolitics in Milton's Mask   45
    Melissa E. Sanchez

Dagon as Queer Assemblage: Effeminacy and   62
Terror in *Samson Agonistes*
    Drew Daniel

An Apology for Queering Milton   88
    Response by *Victoria Silver*

An Introduction Justifying Queer Ways

WILL STOCKTON

In *Tetrachordon*, Milton resoundingly rejects as "crabbed" Augustine's opinion "that manly friendship in all other regards had bin a more becoming solace for Adam, then to spend so many secret years in an empty world with one woman" (1032-33).¹ The relationship of husband and wife, Milton explains (echoing other Protestant writers on marriage), affords more "peculiar comfort[s]" of "company" than those of "the genial bed": "in no company so well as where the differente sexe in most resembling unlikeness, and most unlike resemblance cannot but please best and be pleas'd in the aptitude of that variety" (1033).² The chiasmus of "most resembling unlikeness, and most unlike resemblance" locates the frictions of sexual difference at the center of marital desire and its satisfactions. Yet when Adam, in *Paradise Lost*, asks God for "fellowship . . . / . . . fit to participate / All rational delight" (8.389-91), does he expect God to create another man?³ Adam's citation of the "Lion with Lioness" (8.393) as one of creation's fit "pairs" (8.394) suggests that he understands his "human consort" (8.392) will be female – a being whom he, asleep, sees God fashion as "Manlike, but different sex" (8.471). Feminist criticism of Milton's epic has nonetheless differed sharply over whether God actually delivers the being for which Adam tells Raphael he asked, and the being that Adam claims God promised: "Thy likeness, thy fit help, thy other self, / Thy wish *exactly* to thy hearts desire" (8.450-51, emphasis added).

Rehearsing the many conclusions of both prosecutorial and apologetic readings of Milton's Eve is not necessary, I hope, to make the queer suggestion that Adam's request for companionship stems from a desire audible as homoerotic.⁴ Adam articulates his request for a companion in the discourse of friendship, classically understood as a same-sex relationship among social and intellectual equals.⁵ Seeking "Collateral love, and dearest amitie" (8.425), he asks God, "Among unequals what societie / Can sort, what harmonie or true delight" (8.383-84)? He stresses sameness as he asks God to grant him "Like of his like" (8.423), a copy of himself with whom he can make other copies. He says nothing about the lioness's subordination or inferiority to, or otherwise meaningful difference from, the lion. Recalling for the reader Eve's poolside education in the difference between Adam and her reflection in the water – a story that begins with Eve's own observation that Adam "Like consort to [him]self canst no where find" (4.448) – Adam asks for another version of himself whose degree of difference thereafter becomes a subject of his education. The fact that Adam tells this story to Raphael, whose company Adam admits to relishing (8.210-16), and once Eve has taken leave of the conversation, suggests that Adam's present difficulties negotiating sexual difference both prompt and retroject his wish for friendship. Riven by his understanding of himself as, as well as his current desire to be, Eve's superior, and, as he subsequently confesses, by his companionate but conflicting sense that Eve "so absolute . . . seems / And in her self compleat" (8.547-48), Adam (one historian among many in the poem) arguably reconstructs his initial desire for a consort as a desire ignorant of the difference sexual difference makes. Worries over the relationship between subordination and inferiority, over degrees of similitude among humans, are symptomatically absent in Adam's "initial" request for another version of himself: a homo.

Here at the outset of several essays that collectively seek to justify – that is, to make a case for the critical rightness of while simultaneously producing – queer readings of Milton's work, I would like to suggest that Milton's most famous effort, *Paradise Lost*, raises but does not foreclose a set of queer possibilities for the sexual "orientations" of Adam and Eve. I intend this suggestion as part of my own brief, introductory take on the relative paucity of queer criticism about a poet who focuses his epic-to-end-all-epics on the story of the first "heterosexual" couple (Adam and Eve, not Adam and Steve), but who endows each partner with palpable, entirely extra-Biblical homoerotic longing. Certainly this critical paucity has much to do with what Drew Daniel describes in his contribution as the conservative "tenor of Milton scholarship," with its "constitutive anxiety about 'ruining the sacred truths' and [its] vexed awareness of the watchful paternal gaze of an authorial super-ego." Howsoever patriarchal, Milton's championship of companionate, heterosexual marriage in the divorce tracts and *Paradise Lost* ranks high among these sacred truths threatened by any queer outing of Adam and Eve as homosexuals. At the risk of ruination, I would nonetheless like to proceed with the possibility that Adam and Eve are not in fact heterosexuals, if by that anachronistic term we mean people whose desire tends primarily toward the "opposite" sex.[6]

Alternative possibilities for Adam and Eve's sexual orientations consolidate in the poem under the sign of the homo. For modern readers, this sign includes the homosexual as an equally anachronistic designation for a person whose sexual desire tends primarily toward members of the same sex. As I derive the expanded term from Leo Bersani, however, homoeroticism also marks an erotic orientation toward sameness, including self-sameness, or the appearance of being without a constitutive lack healed only in a dyadic relationship.[7] Adam's attraction to Raphael, who admits to no crippling sense of self-alienation, provides one example of such homoerotic attraction, as does Adam's attraction to (expressed as awe of) God as "One" (8.421) without "deficience found"(8.416). Doubtless the most critically discussed example of homoeroticism in the poem is Eve's attraction to the aquatic reflection of herself that she does not know lacks the "depth" that now so ubiquitously metaphorizes subjectivity. But another example of the same homoerotic orientation is Adam's otherwise heterosexual perception of Eve as "in her self compleat." Raphael's reply to this confession with a lecture on male self-esteem entirely misses the point that Adam has been trying to make to this comparatively self-complete "man" about human deficiency and the need for amity. Whether because Adam will not allow her to or she is truly not fit to, Eve has not satisfied Adam's doubly homoerotic and contradictory desires: for an equal to "solace his defects" (8.419) and for a companion who is not defective.

Persistently frustrating Adam and Eve's homoerotic desires in *Paradise Lost* is a Neoplatonic ontology of the human as constitutionally incomplete, divided in half with the other half to be found across a sexual divide that is also a slope. In the form of "one flesh" heterosexual sociality that Adam and Eve should model according to, among others, Adam himself, each lacks the companionship of the other with whom each also exists in a hierarchal relationship. Adam and Eve are each other's "other half" (4.488), in Adam's words, and he is "her Head" (8.574), in Raphael's.[8] As Bersani argues, however, homoeroticism contains within it a "potentially revolutionary inaptitude . . . for sociality as it is known."[9] If, from the prosecutorial perspective on Eve, the Son most concisely articulates sociality as it is known in *Paradise Lost* when he tells Adam that "God set thee above her made of thee / And for thee, whose perfection farr excell'd / Hers in all real dignitie" (10.148-51), then the homoerotic desires Adam and Eve nevertheless articulate mark the first couple's potentially revolutionary inaptitude for a divinely prescribed heterosocial life. These desires suggest that like Bersani's homos, Adam and Eve might, even before the fall *and without falling* (an event that hinges only and always only on violating that "One easie prohibition" [4.433] against eating from the Tree of Life), make "the politically unacceptable and politically indispensible choice of an outlaw existence."[10]

Let us speculate – for what is the poem itself if not a grand act of speculation, one that repeatedly calls attention to its own speculative status?[11] An Adam and Eve who never turn themselves into the law might never become a couple. An outlaw Adam might still long for the "*fellow*ship" God reportedly promised but never delivered. Or – a conjunction that, in Miltonic contexts, as Peter Herman has taught us, also carries the sense of *and* – he might refuse the misogynistic construction of Eve as his inferior.[12] An outlaw Eve might refuse to frame retroactively her first experience of desire as narcissistically "vain" (4.466). Her desire might tend more toward what we now call lesbianism, if not, even more so than the lonely Adam's, toward autoerotism. After all, Eve's account of learning how "beauty is excelld by manly grace / And wisdom, which alone is truly fair" (4.490-91) testifies *not* to her successful conversion away from an image she must be told "is thy self" (4.468), but instead to the *failure* of that conversion. Eve is so scarcely convinced by the lesson about proper image reflection and other halves that she feels compelled to rehearse it in all its painful detail. These details include her initial turning away from Adam and back toward the pool. They include Adam's proprietary interpellation of her as an individual – not one-in-one but half-in-one – part of himself: "Henceforth an individual solace dear; / Part of my Soul I seek thee, and thee *claim* / My other half" (4.486-88). And they include Adam's supplementation of his proprietary claim with taming force: his "gentle hand / Seisd" hers (4.488-89, emphasis added). Given that Eve's story of sexual conversion makes up the bulk of her very first speech in the poem, one might wonder how often she tells it. How much time has passed since she "yielded" (4.489) and began learning her lesson in heterosocialization? How much time will have to pass before she no longer feels the need to rehearse this lesson? How long before her outlaw desire will so succumb to the law of manly grace's superiority to female beauty that the desire itself will disappear and the law itself will need no articulation?

We know that Satan recognizes the incompleteness of Eve's heterosocialization because he tempts her with the promise that by eating from a tree he slyly tropes as the feminine "Mother of Science" (9.680), she too will possess the cognitive faculties necessary "not onely to discerne / Things in thir Causes, but to trace the wayes / Of highest Agents, deemd however wise" (9.681-83). In other words, she will be "fit to participate / All rational delight" with Adam, and then some. The possibility that Eve may already be as perfectly fit as Adam, and that she is only told otherwise by the misogynists around her, is one point on which a queer reading can build on a feminist one. In this queer reading, Satan tempts Eve with her persistent homoerotic attraction to a reflection of self that she has not been permitted to possess. Although sexual difference remains caught in a hierarchical frame, such that Eve will become wiser than Adam, it is both to Eve's queer credit that she succumbs to this temptation and all the more tragic that she regrets it. Her temptation evinces that her homoerotic attraction to a self undefined by lack retains a psychic priority in her with respect to the hierarchical heterosexual relationship she is currently in that degrades her as the inferior partner.

Adam, too, eventually makes an outlaw choice and regrets it. Yet he does not predicate his choice on a rejection of the doctrine of other halves he previously and literally espoused. Quite the contrary: this doctrine, he feels, compels his disobedience:

> So forcible within my heart I feel
> The Bond of Nature draw me to my owne,
> My own in thee, for what thou art is mine;
> Our State cannot be severd, we are one,
> One Flesh; to loose thee were to loose my self. (9.955-59)

Confounded in his desire once again, Adam voices the frictional principles of marital sameness ("we are one") and possession ("my owne"), and his fall only exacerbates the misogyny entwined in this belief in dyadic self-completion through wedded property. In book ten Adam viciously laments that God did not "fill the World at once / With Men as Angels without Feminine" (10.892-93). Adam is wrong, according to the narrator, about angelic sex. Angels are neither men nor women; they "either Sex assume, or both" (1.424). Presuming the narrator is right, and that Raphael and Michael serve as angelic spokes"men" on issues of sex and gender, the reason all angels assume male form in the poem, however, may well have something to do with the angels' own misogyny. Educating Adam in future history, Michael manifests this misogyny somewhat schizophrenically by attributing death to "th' inabstinence of Eve" (11.476) and then turning on Adam when Adam, as if trying to repeat the lesson of his teacher, attributes "the tenor of Mans woe" (11.632) to "Woman" (11.633). The attribution for this woe then properly belongs, Michael says, recalling the Son's claim that Adam "did'st resign [his] Manhood" (10.148), to "Mans effeminate slackness . . . / . . . who should better hold his place / By wisdome and superiour gifts receav'd" (11.634-36). Responsibility for the fall, the reader may gather, lies not with Eve, except when it does. And it lies not with Adam, except when it does because he is insufficiently manly.

Perhaps most crucial to any attempt at a summary accounting of *Paradise Lost*'s final word on sexual relationality is the fact that Michael gets his own final word about Eve wrong. He instructs Adam to "waken Eve" (12.594), implying that she is asleep, but Adam finds her "wak't" (12.608). If Michael gets this most basic of facts wrong, how much more likely is it that, from the skeptical perspective the reader may occupy in regards to this highly speculative poem, Michael gets his already confused prescription of misogynistic heterosexuality wrong too? Moreover, if Michael's factual wrongs as an angel point upward to what many readers, including most recently Peter Herman and Michael Bryson, have argued is the poem's profound unease with its own representation of God, how much more likely is it that the doctrine of heterosexual misogyny that Raphael, Michael, the Son, Adam, and even Eve preach is entirely fabricated as part and parcel of God's perhaps tyrannical strategy of human subjectivization?[13] How much more likely is it, in short, that the paradise actually lost in the poem is one in which Adam and Eve had the chance to decouple sexual difference from sexual hierarchy and live their lives as sexual outlaws while *still* not breaking that one easy prohibition, that silly little rule about fruit eating, that is the only hard and fast law God has given them – the only law whose violation could get them ejected from Eden?

II

To allow for the possibility that Adam and Eve's relationship need not have lapsed into misogynistic and proprietary heterosexuality, to claim that the poem explores the possibility for different outcomes, and sets up the possibility for counterfactual histories, is not necessarily, or not simply, to join with the apologists in framing this form of heterosexuality as the object of Milton's critique.[14] It is to reframe the poem itself as an open-ended exploration of multiple forms of sexuality – a queer exploration because it entertains the disjunction of sexual desire from the divine prescriptions and narrative teleology that ostensibly govern it. Queer, here, does not simply mean non-normative, nor can it be divorced from perversions of sex and gender.[15] Queerness tracks anti-heteronormative modes of desire, embodiment, and affect. The queer readings in this issue of *Early Modern Culture* thereby extend previous lines of inquiry – many of them feminist, a few explicitly gay or queer – into the unstable formations of gender and sexuality in Milton's work. I have implicitly drawn, for instance, on the long critical conversation about Eve's poolside dalliance that includes James Holstun's reading of it as a demonstration of "the passage of lesbian desire into an inarticulate silence."[16]

An Introduction Justifying Queer Ways

Writing in 1987, slightly before the queer turn in Early Modern Studies, Holstun does not use the word *queer*, but the word nonetheless accommodates his claim that Adam and Eve's relationship "registers [lesbianism's] continuing repressed presence."[17] Same-sex attraction is also the object of the first (I think) markedly queer reading of Milton: Gregory Bredbeck's argument that *Paradise Regain'd* declines an easy exegetical opportunity to condemn sodomy and admits desire's homoerotic pull through Satan's temptation of the Son with "Tall stripling youths" (2.352).[18] More of this past work is worth surveying for the sake of beginning to chart the genealogy of queer Milton criticism to which this issue makes a sustained contribution. Of course, this chart will be incomplete, even as the essays that follow supplement it with their own critical engagements.

Miltonic queerness *qua* homoeroticism is not confined to the two epics. Some of Milton's early work addresses male same-sex desire, too. Focusing on the "unexpressive nuptiall Song" (176) heard by the sinking Lycidas, Bruce Boehrer has read Milton's poem about Edward King as a homoerotic epithalamion.[19] In an essay entitled "Milton's Queer Choice," Ross Leasure has argued that the libertine god presents as much of a sexual threat to the brothers as to the Lady.[20] Milton's friendship with Charles Diodati has also attracted considerable biographical speculation. The friendship prompted verse that, according to Milton, was an inadequate form of conveyance for the intensity of his love:

> Carmine scire velis quâm te redamémque colámque,
> Crede mihi vix hoc carmine scire queas.
> Nam neque noster amor modulis includitur arctis,
> Nec venit ad claudos integer ipse pedes. ("Elegia sexta," 5-8)
>
> [If you do want to learn through my verse how warmly I
> love you, how dearly I cherish you, that, believe me, you
> won't learn through this song, for my love cannot be bound
> in tight-fitting metrics, and, being healthy, does not come to
> you on limping elegiac feet.]

Partly on the basis of such verse, John T. Shawcross has concluded that Diodati was a homosexual, while Milton possessed a "latent homosexualism that was probably repressed consciously (as well as subconsciously) from being overt, except *perhaps* with Diodati."[21] Another recent biographer, Anna Beer, is more psychologically circumspect. She does not deny the homoerotic connection between the two men, but draws instead on scholarship about male friendship in the Renaissance to identify their love as one that "can provide unique intellectual and spiritual," if not necessarily sexual, "fulfillment."[22]

Whether or to what extent Milton was a homosexual is a question that most self-identified queer critics would cast as beside the point. The awkward clinicalism of "latent homosexualism" should remind us that this question is an anachronistic one anyway. The queer point – or one of them, at least – is the more deconstructive one that heteroerotic and homoerotic, normative and perverse, desires frequently intertwine, sometimes switching places, sometimes dissolving the difference between themselves. One of the more familiar sites of temptation for this queer, deconstructive criticism, and the subject of Stephen Guy-Bray's essay in this issue, is Raphael's answer to Adam's question in *Paradise Lost* about how angels "thir Love / Express" (8.615-16):

> Whatever pure thou in the body enjoy'st
> (And pure thou wert created) we enjoy
> In eminence, and obstacle find none
> Of membrane, joynt, or limb, exclusive barrs:
> Easier then Air with Air, if Spirits embrace,
> Total they mix, Union of Pure with Pure
> Desiring; nor retrain'd conveyance need
> As Flesh to mix with Flesh, or Soul with Soul. (8.622-629)

This answer raises a host of questions. How "pure" are Adam and Eve, and are they less pure now than when they were first created? Does Raphael know how Adam and Eve have sex? (The conditional "whatever" suggests he may not.) Do Adam and Eve have sex, and what does that sex look like: is it a conjunction of flesh or the soul, or some combination of both?[23] Is it procreative, and does procreation have to be the primary purpose of sex? Considering that neither the apparent sex of one's partner nor monogamous commitments apparently bound angelic sex, and that Raphael imagines Adam and Eve possibly evolving "to Spirit" (5.497), is monogamous, married, heterosexual sex really the only form of human sexual expression the poem endorses? Considering that all the angels appear to humans as men, does Milton authorize us to envision heaven as a gay orgy? Do we need his authorization? Is Guy-Bray right to argue, as he does here, that the poem is at some level actually promoting sodomy, or non-reproductive sex between men or unsexed beings?

In his *Preface to* Paradise Lost, C.S. Lewis reacted to Raphael's description of angelic sex with the assurance that Milton had no homosexual agenda, although he certainly overstepped the boundaries of good taste:

> The trouble is, I think, that since these exalted creatures are all spoken of by masculine pronouns, we tend, half consciously, to think that Milton is attributing to them a life of homosexual promiscuity. That he was poetically imprudent in raising a matter which invites such a misconception I do not deny; but the real meaning is certainly not filthy, and certainly not foolish. As angels do not die, they need not breed. They are therefore not sexed in the human sense at all. An Angel is, of course, always He (not She) in human language, because whether the male is, or is not, the superior sex, the masculine is certainly the superior gender.[24]

An Introduction Justifying Queer Ways

This misogynistic defense of Milton's hetero credentials ("the masculine is certainly the superior gender") hardly resolves the erotic possibilities that Raphael's account of angelic sex presents. Helping set the ideologically stabilizing agenda of what Herman describes as the dominant paradigm of Milton criticism now exemplified by Stanley Fish's argument that the poem disciplines its reader's errors, Lewis insists on a "real meaning" that forecloses the queer (filthy, foolish) one Guy-Bray perceives. Guy-Bray is not alone in his perverse reading, however, nor, as the queer version of Milton's one just man, would he necessarily be wrong if he were. Jonathan Goldberg has read Raphael's account of angelic sex as "undeniably homo" – and "where likeness is sameness," where "the hierarchies that rank angels . . . are completely absent."25 Looking to the future, Raphael's account also anticipates a time when, according to Goldberg, "all will be all and differences will no longer obtain."26 I would add only that the "perhaps" and "may" in Raphael's evolutionary forecast ("perhaps / Your bodies may at last turn all to Spirit" [5.496- 97]) suggest the limits of the angel's knowledge about divine will and the nature of human beings, including human sexuality. The angel might be wrong about human evolution, as well as about the differences that divide male and female. He might be wrong that Eve is "Less excellent" (8.566) than Adam. By Raphael's own patriarchal standards that place men on top, the sex Adam and Eve are already having may already be homo – a mutual mixture of selves that is, when measured against the angel's prescription, queer.

In a recent article, Karma deGruy follows Goldberg in arguing for the need to critically displace human bodies – caught between the fallen binaries of male and female, superior and inferior – from the center of the poem's focus on gender and sexuality. By "rescuing erotic desire from the realm of the fallen and fleshy" through the model of the angels, deGruy maintains, "Milton does go some way toward . . . envision[ing] a world in which the 'female' and the 'fleshly' are perhaps not always locked into a hierarchically inferior position relative to the 'male' and the 'spiritual'[.]"27 For our purposes here, DeGruy's summary finding that for Milton "paradise meant possibility," coupled with Guy-Bray's argument that the poem promotes sodomy, implies yet another justification for queering Milton beyond the imaginative recovery of prelapsarian and angelic erotic possibilities.28 Linking poetic envisioning to more "practical" enactment, queer Milton criticism may also work to resist the postlapsarian consignment of these possibilities to the realm of the lost. Queer Milton criticism, that is, may locate *Paradise Lost* and Milton's other work in a class of Renaissance texts that James Bromley argues foreground "failures of intimacy" – failures to the extent that their instructions about how to desire do not coalesce around the monogamous, heterosexual couple. "Empowering readers to reimagine their own erotic lives," Bromley contends, many Renaissance "literary texts offer a counterdiscourse to the period's marital advice and conduct books and other texts that attempt to naturalize the consolidation of intimacy around monogamous coupling." Crucial for the purpose of extending this thesis to Milton's work is Bromley's claim that this "counterdiscourse is present even when texts ostensibly demonize alternative forms of intimacy, as a greater flexibility in Renaissance narrative allowed readers to resist what appears to be a textual foreclosure on transgressive intimate practices."²⁹ Throughout his poetry and his prose, Milton contends with competing discourses of erotic intimacy that the reader, both Renaissance and modern, can seize upon to resist the sex education lesson ostensibly proffered. Queers, after all, have long had to resist sex education programs that demonize their forms of erotic life, that associate these forms of life with depression, suicide, disease, and, of course, a violation of God's will.

Read for its counterdiscourses of intimacy, *Paradise Lost* becomes a poem that, at times the reader may choose to privilege, celebrates non-monogamous erotic encounters between multiple unsexed or all-male beings. It allows that Adam and Eve's relationship might have been a truly egalitarian one rather than an alternatively brutal and gently misogynistic one. And, to be sure, it allows that their relationship may still be such an egalitarian one – that "hand in hand" (12.648) equality may lie in their future as well.³⁰ It allows, too, that Adam might have been happier in Eden with Steve rather than Eve, and asks the reader to consider whether this homoerotic desire is necessarily tethered to a misunderstanding of sexual difference. It imagines an Eve who, no inferior to Adam, also might have been happier with another woman, if not alone with herself. It imagines sex, lots of it, and lots of different kinds of it, and not all of it, or any of it, procreative. And it rejects all attempts to foreclose these possibilities as efforts to "straighten out" a poem whose pleasures result from its indulgence in and entertainment of desires it does not succeed in disciplining.

Uninfluenced by this introduction, the essays that follow take their own solitary yet still companionate queer ways. In "'Fellowships of Joy': Angelic Union in *Paradise Lost*," the essay I already previewed the most here, Stephen Guy-Bray argues that Milton's poem privileges not reproductive heterosexuality, which is associated with Satan, Sin and Death, but rather "an unreproductive and ultimately ungendered sexuality that we can only call queer." For Guy-Bray, Milton's representation of angelic sex develops the Renaissance discourse of male friendship as the highest form of affective bonding – a discourse also structuring the poem's long conversation between Adam and Raphael. Marriage between men and women is at best a metaphorical approximation of this more perfect form of same-sex union, which, in the period, is also recognizable as sodomy. Guy-Bray's method of queering Milton is thus, in part, one of inversion: transforming the poet into a proponent of a form of sexuality widely regarded as sinful, and remaking Milton as a poet who himself reinvents sin as the most perfect form of sexual expression.

In "Eros and Anteros: Queer Mutuality in Milton's *Doctrine and Discipline of Divorce*," David Orvis directly challenges the assumption, upon which I relied at the beginning of this introduction, that same-sex friendship provides Milton with the model of relationality that underwrites an ideal heterosexual marriage. Orvis argues that Milton's Anteros does not represent friendship, as critics have traditionally interpreted him; nor is Anteros simply identical to, or distinct from, Eros. As Orvis traces the relationship between Eros and Anteros from classical to modern culture, he finds it tangled up in a confusion of mistaken identities and allegorical and anti-allegorical readings. Drawing on a formulation of queerness as that which opposes coherent sexual signification, Orvis argues that Milton uses this confusion to configure marriage as a potential threat to a form of love that has no name – a love whose queerness lies in its ineffability, in the fact that it can only be defined by what it is not.

Instead of turning Milton into a champion of queerness, the next two essays take seriously Milton's hostility to the queer – queering Milton by exploring, in the first case, his flight from rationality in his defense of chastity, and in the second case, his hero's provoking resemblance to the queer enemy. In "'What Hath Night to Do with Sleep?': Bestial Sex and Human Temporality in *A Mask*," Melissa Sanchez draws on recent conversations about queer time (the relationship of queerness to chronological time and narratives of human development), as well as recent conversations in animal studies, to claim that the boundary between human and animal in *A Mask* is one of temporality, not ontology. Comus tempts the Lady with pleasure now – a pleasure she resists, and a temptation she endures, in the name of a marital chastity that preserves her humanity and prevents her transformation into a beast. Yet the Lady does not clearly win her argument with Comus, as the brothers interrupt the argument with their bungled rescue attempt. Chastity's ultimate defense, Sanchez deduces, lies beyond reason, in spiritual aid figured in the forms of Sabrina and the Attendant Spirit. This aid, in turn, undoes the very distinctions between human reason and animalistic passion underwriting the Lady's defense of chastity.

Drew Daniel's concluding essay, "Dagon as Queer Assemblage: Effeminacy and Terror in *Samson Agonistes*," enters the fray about Milton's endorsement of religious terrorism to posit that a resemblance between Samson as an emasculated male and Dagon as a monstrous hybrid or "queer assemblage" provokes Samson's razing of the Philistine temple. An expansive and meditative essay that weaves together Jasbir Puar's work on terrorism and early modernist work on effeminacy, "Dagon as Queer Assemblage" attends to the negative affects of shame and anxiety that most frequently characterize Milton's attitude toward queer sexualities and toward sodomy in particular. Evidence for Milton's anxious aversion to sodomy appears in his prose, where he further links it to forms of monstrous hybridity that Dagon materializes. (Whereas Guy-Bray's Milton "endorses" sodomy as non-reproductive sex, Daniel's Milton characterizes sodomy as frighteningly, demonically reproductive.) In a section on "the clash of civilizations" between Milton and queer studies, Daniel suggests that analyzing the manifestations and effects of this anxiety, including anxiety's transformation into terror, should be one objective of a queer Milton studies that seeks to do more than recover positive representations of homoerotic and other non-heteronormative relations.

Justifying queer ways of reading Milton, the essays that follow demonstrate particular analytical purchases the concept of queerness can make on just some recurrent questions in Milton studies. What forms does sex take among the angels and among humans before the fall? What is the relationship between friendship and marriage? What does Milton mean by chastity? Does *Samson Agonistes* endorse religious terrorism? Attending to these questions leads to dalliances with others. Is Milton's Christianity hostile to queer expression? Is it the task of the critic to make Milton's work ideologically coherent? And why has

Queer Milton

Milton Studies been so far relatively unaffected by the queer turn in Early Modern (especially Shakespeare) Studies? It is no accident, perhaps, that the five early modernists who collaborate here to raise questions about Milton's queerness are not, like our respondent Victoria Silver, principally Miltonists. For within Early Modern Studies, to twist Satan's famous observation, Milton Studies is its own place. For many of those on the inside, it is a heaven of devotees to the most profound English poet of the seventeenth century. For many of those on the outside, it is a hell of ideological conservatives who have made a career out of committing the intentional fallacy.[31] Whether Milton Studies remains such a divided place depends in part on whether it can accommodate the queers.

Notes

1. All parenthetical references to Milton's works are taken from *The Riverside Milton*, ed. Roy Flannagan (Boston: Houghton Mifflin, 1998).

2. On Milton's opinion about the companionate, rather than simply procreative, purpose of Eve's creation, see James Grantham Turner, *One Flesh: Paradisal Marriage and Sexual Relations in the Age of Milton* (Oxford: Oxford University Press, 1987), 105-06.

3. I have asked this question in a previous essay, "Adam and Eve and the Failure of Heterosexuality," *Queer Renaissance Historiography: Backward Gaze*, eds. Vin Nardizzi, Stephen Guy-Bray, and Will Stockton (Farnham: Ashgate, 2009), 207-28. I conjectured in that essay that, when he made the request, Adam was unaware of "sexual hierarchy – the inequality that is, for Milton, fully constitutive of the difference between human men and women" (215). Assuming now that Milton's agenda in the poem is not so resolutely misogynistic, I would like to pose this question again in a way that holds open the possibility for Adam and Eve to practice various forms of "homosexuality."

4. I borrow the distinction between apologetic and prosecutorial readings from Karen Edwards, "Resisting Representation: All About Milton's Eve," *Exemplaria* 9.1 (1997): 231-53.

5. See Gregory Chaplin, "One Flesh, One Heart, One Soul: Renaissance Friendship and Miltonic Marriage," *Modern Philology* 99.2 (2001): 260-92; and Thomas H. Luxon, *Single Imperfection: Milton, Marriage, Friendship* (Pittsburgh: Duquesne University Press, 2005).

6. On the problems that the concept of heterosexuality causes in understanding early modern forms of desire, see Rebecca Ann Bach, *Shakespeare and Renaissance Literature Before Heterosexuality* (New York: Palgrave Macmillan, 2007).

7. Leo Bersani, *Homos* (Cambridge: Harvard University Press, 1995). On "homo" as a term that connects like to like across chronological divides that ostensibly disallow these connections, see Jonathan Goldberg and Madhavi Menon, "Queering History," *PMLA* 120.5 (2005): 1608-17.

8. On the tensions in and violent consequences of this one flesh model, see Frances E. Dolan, *Marriage and Violence: The Early Modern Legacy* (Philadelphia: University of Pennsylvania Press, 2008).

9. Bersani, *Homos*, 76 (original emphasis).

10. Bersani, *Homos*, 76.

11. This call begins with the narrator's bold but anxious invocation to the muse: "What in me is dark / Illumin" (1.22- 23), an illumination without which the poem is *mere* speculation. The invocation to book 3 is fraught with similar anxiety about the veracity of representation, as the narrator seeks to "see and tell / Of things invisible to mortal sight" (3.55-56). The description of Eden is speculative, too: "if Art could tell" (4.236).

12. See Peter C. Herman, "*Paradise Lost*, the Miltonic 'Or,' and the Poetics of Incertitude," in *Destabilizing Milton: Paradise Lost and the Poetics of Incertitude* (New York: Palgrave Macmillan, 2005), 43-59. The speculation in which I am indulging, as well as the queer challenges

to the "sacred truths" I am encouraging, are broadly congruent with what Herman and others have described as the goal of the "New Milton Criticism" to recast Milton as a poet of uncertainty rather than certainty, of problem-raising rather than problem-solving. See Peter C. Herman and Elizabeth Sauer, eds., *The New Milton Criticism* (Cambridge: Cambridge University Press, 2012).

13. Peter C. Herman, "Incertitude, Authority, and Milton's God," in *Destabilizing Milton*, 107-25; Michael Bryson, *The Atheist Milton* (Farnham: Ashgate, 2012), 93-107.

14. On the queerness of counterfactuals, see Kathryn Schwarz, "Queer Futility: Or, The Life and Death of *King John*," *Shakesqueer: A Queer Companion to the Complete Works of Shakespeare*," ed. Madhavi Menon (Durham: Duke University Press, 2011), 167.

15. For a critique of the use of queerness as a synonym for non-normative, see Sharon Marcus, "Queer Theory for Everyone: A Review Essay," *Signs* 31.1 (2005): 196-97; and my review of Madhavi Menon's *Shakesqueer*, "Shakespeare and Queer Theory," *Shakespeare Quarterly* 63.2 (2012): 224-35.

16. James Holstun, "'Will You Rent Our Ancient Love Asunder?: Lesbian Elegy in Donne, Marvell, and Milton," *English Literary History* 54.4 (1987): 836.

17. Holstun, "'Will You Rent Our Ancient Love Asunder?," 837.

18. Gregory Bredbeck, "Milton's Sodomite," in *Sodomy and Interpretation: Marlowe to Milton* (Ithaca: Cornell University Press, 1991), 189-31. For a continuation of the discussion about the "Tall stripling youths," see Philip Rollinson, "The Homoerotic Aspect of Temptation in *Paradise Regained*," *English Language Notes* 32.2 (1995): 31-35; Claude J. Summers, "The (Homo)Sexual Tradition in Milton's *Paradise Regained*," *Reclaiming the Sacred: The Bible in Gay and Lesbian Culture*, ed. Raymond-Jean Frontain (New York: Haworth, 1997), 45-46; John T. Shawcross, "Milton's *Paradise Regain'd* and the Second Temptation," *ANQ* 21 (2008): 34-41; and David V. Urban, "The Homosexual Temptation of the Son in Milton's *Paradise Regained*: A Reply to John T. Shawcross and Claude J. Summers," *Connotations* 21.2-3 (2011/2012): 272-77 (www.connotations.uni-tuebingen.de/urban02123.htm).

19. Bruce Boehrer, "'Lycidas': The Pastoral Elegy as Same-Sex Epithalamium," *PMLA* 117.2 (2002): 222-36.

20. Ross Leasure, "Milton's Queer Choice: Comus at Castlehaven," *Milton Quarterly* 36.2 (2002): 63-86.

21. John T. Shawcross, *John Milton: The Self and the World* (Lexington: University of Kentucky Press, 2001), 59 (original emphasis).

22. Anna Beer, *Milton: Poet, Pamphleteer, and Patriot* (New York: Bloomsbury Press, 2008), 51. See also, along similar lines, John Rumrich, "The Erotic Milton," *Texas Studies in Literature and Language* 41.2 (1999): 128-41.

23. For the view that Adam and Eve do have bodily sex before the fall, see James Grantham Turner, *One Flesh*; and Peter Lindenbaum, "Lovemaking in Milton's Paradise," *Milton Studies* 6 (1974): 277-306. Kent R. Lenhof argues to the contrary in "Nor turnd I weene": *Paradise Lost* and Pre-Lapsarian Sexuality, *Milton Quarterly* 34.3 (2000): 67- 84; as does Thomas H. Luxon in "Milton's Wedded Love," in *Single Imperfection*, 123-56. In "How Human Life Began: Sexual Reproduction in Book 8 of *Paradise Lost*," in *Sex Before Sex: Figuring the Act in Early Modern England*, eds. James Bromley and Will Stockton (Minnesota: University of Minnesota Press, 2013), 263-90, however, Luxon argues that conversation, especially between Raphael and Adam and Adam and God, constitutes one mode of prelapsarian sex. Given queer theory's interest in what constitutes sex in the first place, this question of what sex is prior to the ontological divisions and ruptures occasioned by the fall seems ripe for further queer inquiry.

24. C.S. Lewis, *A Preface to "Paradise Lost*," (Oxford: Oxford University Press, 1961), 112-13.

25. Jonathan Goldberg, *The Seeds of Things: Theorizing Sexuality and Materiality in Renaissance Representations* (New York: Fordham University Press, 2009), 194.

26. Goldberg, *The Seeds of Things*, 195.

27. Karma deGruy, "Desiring Angels: The Angelic Body in *Paradise Lost*," *Criticism* 54.1 (2012): 142.

28. deGruy, "Desiring Angels," 43.

29. James M. Bromley, *Intimacy and Sexuality in the Age of Shakespeare* (Cambridge: Cambridge University Press, 2012), 2.

30. See also Lee Morrissey's argument that Eve leads the way forward through a paradise they never actually leave because it is "within" (12.587); "Literature and the Postsecular: *Paradise Lost?*," *Religion & Literature* 41.3 (2009): 102-05.

31. Blackwell's *Companion to Aesthetics*, 2nd., ed. Stephen Davies et al. (Oxford: Basil Blackwell, 2009) in fact cites *Paradise Lost* in its defense of the intentional fallacy: "Intention, though undoubtedly a psychological state, ceases to be unavailable to others because it can display itself in action: and since a literary work may be the product of a complex set of actions, it is unclear why we should not see its creator's intentions made manifest in it (as they clearly are in, say, Milton's *Paradise Lost*)" (369). Thanks to Ari Fiedlander for bringing this reference to my attention.

"Fellowships of Joy": Angelic Union in *Paradise Lost*

STEPHEN GUY-BRAY

Since its first publication, many readers of *Paradise Lost* have been struck by the fact that Milton's Adam and Eve have sex before the Fall – or, to use Milton's terminology, that they perform "the Rites / Mysterious of connubial Love" (IV.742-3).[1] In conjunction with his emphasis on the tender closeness of Adam and Eve, Milton's appreciative depiction of prelapsarian human sexuality would seem to establish a standard for human sexuality that is lost with the Fall and, as he goes on to point out, very different from our own experience of sexuality. Adam and Eve in Eden appear to display an original and originating heterosexuality compared to which all postlapsarian sexuality falls short in one way or another or indeed in several. In fact, it might well be the case that Milton characterizes Adam and Eve's connubial rites as mysterious because he wants to suggest that we cannot understand them from our fallen perspective. Nevertheless, Adam and Eve's marriage has typically been understood as an ideal that everyone should follow and historically as a crucial stage in the movement towards companionate marriage.

In this paper I shall argue, however, that not only is the love of Adam and Eve not the first heterosexuality in the poem but also that even before the Fall human sexuality (as opposed to angelic sexuality) is, if not entirely condemned, at least seen as a sign of the imperfect nature of all non-angelic creatures – humans as well as animals. As Raphael points out to Adam, sexual intercourse, which he describes as "the sense of touch whereby mankind / Is propagated" (VIII.579-80), is "voutsaf't / To Cattel and each Beast" (VIII.581-2). In making the connection between sexuality and reproduction, Raphael's comment appears to be exactly what we would expect in a Christian poem, but in the poem itself reproduction is not especially important; to me, Raphael's attitude is more appropriate to sex after the Fall.[2] Kent R. Lehnhof reminds us that "Defoe had trouble accepting sex in the Garden because such sex would necessarily have been perfect, and perfect sex would invariably have ended in conception."[3] I think that Defoe was wrong about what perfect sex is for Milton here: in *Paradise Lost*, only angelic sexuality is perfect. As James Grantham Turner points out, *Paradise Lost* is "virtually unique in ascribing active eroticism, not only to the unfallen Adam and Eve, but to angels both fallen and unfallen."[4] What is more, angelic sex is sex between men, or what would have been called sodomy in Milton's time.[5] Instead of an original and ideal heterosexuality, Milton gives us a non-reproductive and ultimately ungendered sexuality that we can only call queer.

In his presentation of ideal sexuality (or, more precisely if less concisely, ideal expressions of mutual love; for convenience, I shall stick with sexuality in this paper), Milton draws on the very popular tradition going back to the ancient Greeks and still enormously influential in Milton's own time according to which love between men was the highest form of love. In his book on Milton, Thomas H. Luxon argues that in *Paradise Lost* Milton tries "to harness classical friendship theory to the task of reforming heterosexual Christian marriage."[6] I would point out, however, that this is only true of his depiction of Adam and Eve: in Milton's depiction of the angels, we see the purest form of classical friendship, something to which classical writers aspired but which can only be achieved by angels. We also see in the angels the purest form of marriage: when Milton memorably describes marriage as turning two people into "one Flesh, one Heart, one Soule" (VIII.99), we should bear in mind that in the context of *Paradise Lost* Adam and Eve's union (and, of course, all human unions since them) can only appear as an imperfect imitation of the unions that, as Raphael will inform Adam, angels can effortlessly achieve.[7]

Several critics have looked at this topic from the point of view of the classical literature on male friendships, but I think it is useful to consider the possibility that Milton also draws on Renaissance versions of this tradition. In the context of my argument here, I am especially interested in the versions by Edmund Spenser and by Sir Thomas Browne. In Book IV of the *Faerie Queene*, Spenser distinguishes three kinds of love: familial, heterosexual, and male-male. These kinds are presented as a narrative in which a man goes from loving his family to loving a woman – "For naturall affection soone doth cesse, / And quenched is with *Cupids* greater flame" – and ultimately to loving another man: "So loue of soule doth loue of bodie passe."[8] Perhaps particularly interesting for us is that while love of one's family is fleeting, it is also the only kind of love described as "natural": both a man's love for a woman and a man's love for a male friend are tacitly presented as unnatural. As well, familial and heterosexual love are connected in being loves of the body, as opposed to the love of a male friend, which is seen as spiritual. In its presentation of human relationships, the *Faerie Queene* is an important precedent for *Paradise Lost*, but there are clearly some significant differences: familial affection does not exist in Milton's poem (with the exception of the story of Satan and Sin, which I shall discuss below), for instance, and, most crucially, the body / soul dichotomy so important to Spenser's formulation does not apply to Milton's angels.

Milton's presentation of ideal love in *Paradise Lost* is especially close to Sir Thomas Browne's comments on friendship in *Religio Medici*. Like Spenser, Browne assumes that the highest form of human relationship is masculine friendship; unlike Spenser, however, Browne is explicitly concerned with the ways in which even this kind of relationship is less than ideal. In writing of these friendships, Browne states that "united soules are not satisfied with embraces, but desire to be truly each other, which being impossible, their desires are infinite, and must proceed without a possibility of satisfaction."[9] While for Spenser, the "loue of soule" is what characterizes masculine friendship, for Browne it is the wish for absolute identity with the beloved. When Browne returns to the topic later he says that the "part of our loving friends that we love, is not that part that we embrace; but that insensible part that our armes cannot embrace."[10] Browne presents the literal embraces in which we delight as really metaphorical in that they merely represent the ideal conjunction between two souls. In this context, I would argue that it is not especially important whether these embraces are sexual or not: what matters is that when two human bodies touch, this touch simultaneously affirms their connection and their separation. As we shall see, the angelic sexuality of *Paradise Lost* is the logical next step.

Before I look at these ideal conjunctions, however, I want to consider what are for Milton the melancholy consequences of a physical expression of union. The original heterosexuality in Milton's world is not the relationship of Adam and Eve but rather the union of Satan and his offspring Sin. In Book II, Sin tells Satan that when he first plotted against God "shining heav'nly fair, a Goddess arm'd / Out of thy head I sprung" (II.757-8). While the angels at first found her repellent she eventually became attractive, especially to Satan himself:

> full oft
> Thy self in me thy perfect image viewing
> Becam'st enamour'd, and such joy thou took'st
> With me in secret, that my womb conceiv'd
> A growing burden (II.763-7).

The result of this conception is the birth of Death, and so we see that the original pattern of heterosexuality and of family life is both incestuous and disastrous. What is more, this is a heterosexuality based on similarity and not on difference – something that is arguably true of Adam and Eve themselves as well, since the story of Eve's origin as Adam famously narrates it in Book VIII bears a close resemblance to the story of the origin of Sin and Death.

The story gets worse, of course: once Death is born he rapes his mother and begets "yelling Monsters" (II.795) which "when they list into the womb / That bred them . . . return" (II.798-9). Such, it seems, are the miseries of family life. It will not have escaped the reader's attention that it is Sin, the female figure (and, in fact, the first female figure ever), who suffers most, and it could be argued that her pains are in some sense connected to the punishment pronounced on Eve later in the poem. We could further support an argument that Milton is especially concerned with and especially alarmed by female iniquities by pointing out that the narration of this scene takes place by the side of the abyss Milton describes as

> The Womb of nature, and perhaps her Grave,
> Of neither Sea, nor Shore, nor Air, nor Fire,
> But all these in thir pregnant causes mixt (II.911-13).

In this part of the poem, various kinds of unpleasantness (to put it mildly) are expressed through womb symbolism; the monstrous fertility of Sin is only one of the ways in which horror is expressed through the vagina.

The penis fares no better, however, as Sin's account of the birth of her son, conceived in incest, suggests:

> He my inbred enemie
> Forth issu'd, brandishing his fatal Dart
> Made to Destroy (II.785-7).

The reference to Death as Sin's "inbred enemie" suggests that to be related to someone is at least as likely to produce enmity as amity. Just as Satan and Sin establish a grim precedent for heterosexuality, so the first familial relationship in the poem establishes an equally gloomy precedent for family life, and one that clearly foreshadows Abel's murder, which is shown to Adam near the end of the poem. Similarly, Death's "fatal Dart" – at once the spear with which Death as a warrior does his work and the phallus with which he will repeatedly rape his mother – links the penis not primarily to sexual enjoyment, however one-sided, but rather to reproduction. In other words, it is not the case, as one might expect, that Milton condemns a sexuality unconnected to reproduction but instead that both male and female genitals, in this first ever example of sexual activity, are condemned even when they are used for what was traditionally felt to be their proper purpose.

What is more, the fallen angels are described throughout *Paradise Lost* in terms that suggest tumescence. We see this first when Satan speaks to the fallen angels in the first book and suggests that they cannot "fail to re-ascend / Self-rais'd" (I.633-4), but perhaps the best example comes when Satan responds to Abdiel's reminder that God created them all by saying

> We know no time when we were not as now;
> Know none before us, self-begot, self-rais'd
> By our own quick'ning power (V.859-61).

Here, erection is presented as an image of stubbornness in a bad cause, in the very worst of causes. For these bad angels, the motiveless malignity of their tumescence is both precedent and warrant for a life free of obedience or veneration. If the story of Satan, Death, and Sin has given us a depressing picture of the origins of heterosexuality and family life, what appears to be the autotelic nature of the sexuality of the angels who are soon to fall suggests that there is no alternative – or, rather, that Milton has not given us one yet.

My point here is not that sexual activity in *Paradise Lost* is all bad: Milton explicitly presents sexual activity as one of the blessings of humanity, most notably in the hymn to wedded love (IV.750-75). Nevertheless, I think Milton's imagery throughout the poem demonstrates the dangers of a relation between two people that must take physical expression. Adam himself seems to be to some extent aware that the higher connection is between two souls. For instance, when he first sees Eve he says that man and woman "shall be one Flesh, one Heart, one Soul" (VIII.499) – thus neatly recapitulating Spenser's three types of love – and he tells Raphael that what he values in Eve is not primarily the sexual relation but rather all the things she does "which declare unfeign'd / Union of Mind, or in us both one Soul" (VIII.603-4). Much of the initial description of Adam and Eve in Books

IV and V presents this union very movingly, but later in Book V we have the scene in which Satan asks Beelzebub "Sleepst thou Companion dear" (V.673) and adds

> Thou to me thy thoughts
> Was wont, I mine to thee was wont t'impart;
> Both waking we were one; how then can now
> Thy sleep dissent? (V.676-9).

The language is as moving, the narrative situation very close to the scene earlier in the book in which Eve awakes from her bad dream.[11]

In part, of course, the similarity between these scenes is foreshadowing: Milton wants to suggest that while the closeness between Adam and Eve is one of the best things in the world of the poem, and while it sets a pattern for marital concord to which we should all aspire, it is this very closeness that will bring about Adam's fall after Eve's and because of Eve's. But it is not just foreshadowing. As ethereal beings, the fallen angels still have access to a union to which humans cannot aspire. Milton has already gestured towards this union when he described the ending of the council in Hell:

> O shame to men! Devil with Devil damn'd
> Firm concord holds, men onely disagree
> Of Creatures rational (II.496-8).

Even in hell, then, the fallen angels have a concord – both in couples and as a group – that apparently surpasses human concord of any kind in much the same way, to cite two other examples from Book II, that their musical abilities surpass human abilities and their ability to build Pandemonium surpasses all human architectural feats.

But it is important to note that this infernal union, however superior it may be in many respects to human union, is still only partial. When Satan first sees Adam and Eve we learn something surprising about devils from Satan's reaction:

> Sight hateful, sight tormenting! thus these two
> Imparadis't in one anothers arms
> The happier *Eden*, shall enjoy thir fill
> Of bliss on bliss, while I to Hell am thrust,
> Where neither joy nor love, but fierce desire,
> Among our other torments not the least,
> Still unfulfill'd with pain of longing pines (IV.505-11).

The crucial point here is that the perfect union enjoyed by angels is not purely the relation of soul to soul, not only a disembodied merging of two beings, but also a desire that can be physically expressed and one that gives physical release – and I think that Milton's use of the verb "to thrust" emphasises the physicality of angelic sexuality.

Fellowships of Joy

Of course, the angelic orgasm to which Satan in vain aspires is not like a human orgasm since angelic bodies are not like human bodies. Typically for *Paradise Lost*, we first learn this in a bad context when Milton tells us that fallen angels can turn themselves into male or female spirits:

> For Spirits when they please
> Can either Sex assume, or both; so soft,
> And uncompounded is thir Essence pure,
> Not ti'd or manacl'd with joynt or limb,
> Nor founded on the brittle strength of bones,
> Like cumbrous flesh; but in what shape they choose
> Dilated or condens'd, bright or obscure,
> Can execute thir aerie purposes,
> And works of love or enmity fulfill (I.423-31).

Here, Milton explains how it is that the demons will be known in Biblical times as either Baalim (male) or Ashtaroth (female), and it is really only works of enmity that are at issue.

In the poem itself, however, we only see masculine angels. This is perhaps not surprising, as until the nineteenth century angels were (for the most part) depicted as male, but it is interesting to note that, as Lehnhof has remarked in a superb article on masculinity in *Paradise Lost*, "Adam is the epic's only male."[12] As the passage I have just quoted from Book I makes clear, in *Paradise Lost* what we think of as masculinity and femininity are merely disguises for angels. But as Lehnhof goes on to point out, "the characters in *Paradise Lost* who are not "really" (that is, substantially) male seem secure in their masculinity, while the lone character who is "really" male cannot keep from becoming effeminate."[13] It would seem that the masculinity we know here on Earth is substantial without being real in an important sense, just as – to return to the *Religio Medici* – the substantial embraces we give to our friends (and, by extension, to our lovers) are not real either: as was the case with Browne, we could say that what we take to be literal is revealed to be metaphorical. In Milton's poem, the angels, who have neither bodies nor gender in our sense, epitomize a genuine sex and a genuine sexuality for which we can find only substitutes – the touch which Raphael rather dismissively mentions.

In the poem, our first example of the angelic ability to assume any shape as a work of enmity comes when Satan disguises himself to find out from Uriel the way to Earth:

> And now a stripling Cherub he appeers,
> Not of the prime, yet such as in his face
> Youth smil'd Celestial, and to every Limb
> Sutable grace diffus'd (III.636-9).

I think it is significant that Satan takes the form not only of an angel but, in particular, the form of an especially young and beautiful angel. What is more, I would argue that the passage anticipates the "Tall stripling youths rich clad, of fairer hew / Than *Ganymede* or *Hylas*" who form part of Jesus' temptations in *Paradise Regain'd*.[14] Over the course of *Paradise Lost* we see Satan take other disguises – most notably the serpent – but I want to stress that he begins by assuming male beauty in the form considered most attractive by both Renaissance and classical poets and that he does so in a context that suggests that male beauty is attractive even to the highest of the angels.

Our sense of the power of male beauty in *Paradise Lost* is underlined by Raphael's refulgent beauty when he appears to Adam: as Turner points out, "Raphael's entrance is . . . charged with sexual energy."[15] Nor is it only Raphael's physical manifestation that is sexualized: the long conversation between him and Adam, however full of useful religious doctrine it may be, is presented as a love scene. Admittedly, this view of their conversation is not the conventional one among Miltonists, but there have been some exceptions. Arguing that the scene between Adam and Raphael is the highpoint of the poem's homoeroticism, Linda Gregerson has pointed out that their conversation contains "deliberate invocations of erotic love poetry" and that critics have considered these only as examples of "idealized male 'friendship.'"[16] Even more recently, Jonathan Goldberg has focused on the erotics of this passage, noting, for instance, the connection between Raphael's statement to Adam – "Nor are thy lips ungrateful, sire of men" (VIII.218) – and Milton's comment about Eve's attitude to conversation with Adam just a few lines earlier – "from his lip / Not words alone pleased her" (VIII.56-7).[17]

In the passage I have just cited from Gregerson, the inverted commas around friendship appear to indicate that we should really understand the connection between the man and the angel as sexual, but I would argue that it is crucial to see the connection as both friendly and sexual. Raphael and Adam represent the highest form of masculine friendship: while for Adam, at least, the true connection with his friend of which Browne writes is not possible (or not yet possible: Raphael holds out the hope that humans may eventually become angels), Milton is careful to present the conversation as a meeting of souls that is also an encounter between beautiful men. For me, it is this encounter, rather than the marriage of Adam and Eve, that is the paradigmatic relationship in *Paradise Lost*, if not the ideal one. To return to Spenser is helpful here. Spenser presents masculine friendship as a force that disciplines both familial and marital love: "But faithfull friendship doth them both suppresse, / And them with maystring discipline doth tame."[18] One way to see what happens in *Paradise Lost* is to consider that Adam and Eve's actions have sentenced all their descendents to imperfect and unruly heterosexuality and foreclosed the possibility of the angelic homosexuality Raphael offers to Adam.

As male beauty is the standard of beauty in *Paradise Lost*, so angelic sexual expression is the standard of sexual expression. We learn this when Raphael answers Adam's question about love among angels:

Whatever pure thou in the body enjoy'st

> (And pure thou wert created) we enjoy
> In eminence, and obstacle find none
> Of membrane, joynt, or limb, exclusive barrs:
> Easier then Air with Air, if Spirits embrace,
> Total they mix, Union of Pure with Pure
> Desiring; nor restrain'd conveyance need
> As Flesh to mix with Flesh, or Soul with Soul (VIII.622-9).

The most relevant part of the speech for my purposes here is "Total they mix." Earlier, Raphael explained to Adam that the substance of angelic being is very different from that of humans: "All Heart they live, all Head, all Eye, all Ear, / All Intellect, all sense" (VI.350-1). And all genitals as well then: the union of angel with angel is not the union of soul with soul alone, but a total and mutual interpenetration throughout their beings.

As I pointed out earlier, the highest form of relationship in Renaissance England was masculine friendship, because that was felt to be a relationship between souls. Even there, however, the union cannot be absolute and the embraces we give our friends are only substitutes; as a result, even masculine friends "must proceed without a possibility of satisfaction," to return to Browne's wording. Milton would appear to be making a similar point in implicitly contrasting the imperfections of the marriage of Adam and Eve and the fatal differences between them with angelic unions: after all, in *Paradise Lost*, the highest form of relationship is not the human marriage that takes up so much of the poem but the angelic unions that humans imitate. The marriage of Adam and Eve is the best human relationship possible (and in the context of Renaissance literature Milton is an innovator in giving a heterosexual union this sort of primacy), but as I have already pointed out, in *Paradise Lost* Adam and Eve are not even the first heterosexual couple: that honour is reserved for Satan and Sin. What is more, it is the relationship between Adam and Raphael that is the poem's best relationship. For Milton, while humans apparently cannot escape from heterosexuality, even the marriage so central to church and state can only be an imperfect imitation of heavenly homoeroticism.

When Browne writes that even masculine friends cannot find satisfaction, he means that they cannot achieve a true union; for us now, however, it is tempting to understand satisfaction in a sexual sense and to read this passage as referring to Renaissance prohibitions against sex between men. I mention this because I do not want to be taken to argue that *Paradise Lost* is a manifesto for gay love, however tempting such a conclusion would be. For instance, just as we could argue that the union of Satan and Sin taints heterosexuality, so we could argue that the union of Satan and Beelzebub taints homosexuality. As regards sexuality at least, in *Paradise Lost* the Fall happened before the Fall. Nevertheless, the male-male unions alluded to by Raphael remain the best kind of relationship possible. The theologian Mark Jordan has defined sodomy as "the pure essence of the erotic without connection to reproduction," a definition that perfectly fits the loves of Milton's angels.[19] Measured against this celestial sodomy, human sexuality, whether pre or postlapsarian, whether homosexual or heterosexual, can only fall short. It is in this establishment of same-sex unions as the real thing rather than as belated or imitative or secondary that Milton is not only queer but also, I think, that he manages to queer all of creation.

Notes

1. All references to the works of Milton are to the edition by John Shawcross.
2. In a very good recent discussion of touch in *Paradise Lost*, Joe Moshenska has persuasively argued that although Raphael seems to be an entirely conventional and orthodox commentator on sexual love, we may well see his perspective as limited. See "'Transported Touch,'" especially 3 and 9. Moshenska also points out that Raphael's stress on propagation could seem odd; see 11 *et seq*. Similarly, James Grantham Turner says that 'Raphael is by no means an infallible guide'; see *One Flesh*, 278.
3. Lehnhof, "'Nor turnd I weene,'" 68.
4. Goldberg, *One Flesh*, 53.
5. As angels can assume any form they like – a point Milton makes more than once – other kinds of coupling (and not just coupling) are of course possible. But as Jonathan Goldberg remarks, "The ability of angels to assume whatever form they choose . . . seems realized only in couplings across kind, transformation across gender" (198). When angels interact, they are always male.
6. Luxon, *Single Imperfection*, 3. As the subtitle of Luxon's book indicates, his focus is on friendship and marriage throughout Milton's work; by the time he gets to *Paradise Lost*, however, his focus is almost entirely on Adam and Eve. Good recent treatments of the topic that also neglect the angels are Edwards, "Gender, Sex, and Marriage in Paradise"; and Willie, "Spiritual Union and the Problem of Sexuality."
7. In *The Reformation of the Subject*, Linda Gregerson points out that "the interpenetrating angels are explicitly imagined on the same continuum of desire that comprehends angelic sexuality" (174), so perhaps the imitation will ultimately be successful.
8. Spenser, *Faerie Queene*, IV.ix.2.1-2 and 8.
9. Browne, *Religio Medici*, 131.
10. Ibid, 156.
11. For Goldberg's account of this passage, see *The Seeds of Things*, 196.
12. Lehnhof, "Performing Masculinity in *Paradise Lost*,' 64. Here he cites specifically I.423-31 and VI.350-3.
13. Ibid, 68. See also 65: "the masculinity of these nonmale angels is quite convincing"; here Lehnhof cites X.888-95.
14. *Paradise Regain'd*, II.352-3. For discussions of the homoerotic nature of this temptation, see Bredbeck, Milton's Ganymede"; and Summers, "The (Homo)Sexual Temptation in Milton's *Paradise Regained*."
15. Turner, *One Flesh*, 270. Turner appears to think that the sexiness is for Eve's benefit and the intellectual enlightenment for Adam's.
16. Gregerson, *The Reformation of the Subject*, 174. See 174-5 for Gregerson's discussion of the conversation between Raphael and Adam.
17. See Goldberg, *The Seeds of Things*, 188-95.
18. Spenser, *Faerie Queene*, IV.ix.2.3-4.
19. Jordan, *The Invention of Sodomy in Christian Theology*, 176.

Works Cited

Bredbeck, Gregory. "Milton's Ganymede: Negotiations of Homoerotic Tradition in *Paradise Regain'd*." *PMLA* 106 (1991): 262-76.

Browne, Sir Thomas. *Religio Medici*. London, 1642.

Edwards, Karen. "Gender, Sex, and Marriage in Paradise." In *A Concise Companion to Milton*, ed. Angelica Duran. 144-60. Oxford: Blackwell, 2007.

Goldberg, Jonathan. *The Seeds of Things: Theorizing Sexuality and Materiality in Renaissance Representations*. New York: Fordham University Press, 2009.

Gregerson, Linda. *The Reformation of the Subject: Spenser, Milton, and the English Protestant Epic*. Cambridge: Cambridge University Press, 1995.

Jordan, Mark. *The Invention of Sodomy in Christian Theology*. Chicago: University of Chicago Press, 1998.

Lehnhof, Kent R. "'Nor turnd I weene': *Paradise Lost* and Pre-Lapsarian Sexuality." *Milton Quarterly* 34.3 (2000): 67-83.

-----. 'Performing Masculinity in *Paradise Lost*.' *Milton Studies* 50 (2009): 64-77.

Luxon, Thomas H. *Single Imperfection: Milton, Marriage and Friendship*. Pittsburgh: Duquesne University Press, 2005.

Milton, John. *The Complete Poetry of John Milton*. Ed. John T. Shawcross. New York: Anchor Books, 1971.

Moshenska, Joe. "'Transported Touch': The Sense of Feeling in Milton's Eden." *ELH* 79 (2012): 1-31.

Spenser, Edmund. *Poetical Works*. Ed. J.C. Smith and E. de Selincourt. London: Oxford University Press, 1912.

Summers, Claude J. "The (Homo)Sexual Temptation in Milton's *Paradise Regained*." In *Reclaiming the Sacred: The Bible in Gay and Lesbian Culture*, ed. Raymond-Jean Frontain. 45-69. New York: Haworth Press, 1997.

Turner, James Grantham. *One Flesh: Paradisal Marriage and Sexual Relations in the Age of Milton*. Oxford: Clarendon Press, 1987.

Willie, Rachel. "Spiritual Union and the Problem of Sexuality." *Milton Studies* 47 (2008): 168-84.

Eros and Anteros: Queer Mutuality in Milton's *Doctrine and Discipline of Divorce*

DAVID L. ORVIS

In central London, at the heart of Piccadilly Circus, stands the Shaftesbury Monument Memorial Fountain, a structure commemorating the philanthropic work of Anthony Ashley- Cooper, 7th Earl of Shaftesbury. Atop this monument and cast in aluminum is the statue of a scantily clad youth accoutered with wings and a bow (fig. 1). Although passers-by routinely identify this statue as Eros, the sculptor Alfred Gilbert claims it is Anteros, Eros's brother, since he, "as opposed to Eros or Cupid, the frivolous tyrant," represents "reflective and mature love."[1] Eros, in other words, embodies carnal lust, Anteros a benevolent mutuality transcendent of erotic love. This distinction is lost upon the vast majority of the statue's visitors – a consequence, no doubt, of Eros's prominence among the erotes. Nevertheless, the ease with which one can confuse two figures who purportedly represent two very different kinds of love bespeaks a confusion inherent in the figures themselves and the conceptual differences they supposedly signify. As we shall see, this confusion has a long, complex history, one that stretches back thousands of years before the Shaftesbury Memorial's unveiling. The controversy Anteros tends to engender is nearly as ancient, so perhaps Gilbert half-expected the mixed reactions to his sculpture. While he insisted that the memorial portrays a mature, spiritual love, this explanation did little to assuage critics who thought it in poor taste to immortalize Shaftesbury's philanthropy with a nearly naked youth modeled after Angelo Colarossi, the sculptor's then-fifteen-year-old assistant. In this instance, embodiment appears to have undermined, indeed militated against, a (strictly) Neoplatonic representation of love. Or to put it in literary terms, the tenor could not efface the vehicle, which in any case continues to be misrecognized as Eros, the youthful incarnation of (homo)erotic love.[2]

Eros and Anteros

Figure 1: Anteros, from the Shaftesbury Monument Memorial Fountain. Photograph by David L. Orvis.

Dating back to antiquity, the tradition of Eros and Anteros is conflicted at least in part because it has been subject to the vagaries of diachronic change and synchronic variance. Yet, even the earliest depictions of the erotes seem vexed, as if conflict is bound up in the very notion of Anteros. Whereas in some classical works Anteros is Eros's companion and patron of requited love, in others he is Eros's nemesis and avenger of spurned love. In some texts he is born of heteroerotic love, while in many others he is the product of homoerotic love. And while sometimes Anteros emerges from love requited, at other times he is manifest in love scorned. This cacophony of origins and significations derives from Anteros's name, which taken from the ancient Greek Αντερως can mean anything from "different love," to "opposite love," to "against love" – all of which suggest the possibility of mutuality *as well as* antagonism. For example, does "against love" mean "love pressed against love?" Or does it signify "love pitted against love?" In the first interpretation, Anteros and his brother Eros constitute a mythic same-sex couple; in the second, they are bitter enemies locked in an eternal struggle. The cohabitation of love returned and love scorned presents problems of interpretation that during the Renaissance were compounded by two trends: first, humanist scholars often confused and conflated Anteros not only with Eros, but also with Amor Lethaeus, the dissolver of love (fig. 2); and second, the rise to prominence of Neoplatonism encouraged revisionist readings of the homoerotic tale of Eros and Anteros as exemplifying a spiritual mutuality that transcends carnal desire.[3] Thus, one is never quite sure which of the erotes is being presented. Rather like Michel Foucault's famous description of sodomy, the literature on Eros and Anteros is "utterly confused."[4]

Figure 2: Woodcut showing the erotes, with Eros and Anteros wrestling over the palm, by Filippo Ferroverde, from Vincezo Cartari, Imagini delli Dei de gl'Antichi (Padova: Pietro Paolo Tozzi, 1615), 442. © The Warburg Institute.

One might be surprised, therefore, to find Eros and Anteros among the allusions John Milton includes in his *Doctrine and Discipline of Divorce* (1643) to figure the mutual love and desire that should precede matrimony. Yet, as Will Stockton discusses in his introduction to this special issue, Milton's conceptualizations of companionship (whether hetero or homo) are not, as some critics would have it, consistent. One of the aims of the present essay is to demonstrate that this inconsistency is evident even within his divorce tracts, and hence, too, that Milton continued to wrestle with the concept of matrimonial love even as he tried to make the case for divorce. In *Tetrachordon* (1645), for instance, Milton dismisses Augustine's pronouncement that male friends, rather than mixed-sex spouses, constitute the ideal union:

> *Austin* contests that manly friendships in all other regards had bin a more becomming solace for *Adam*, then to spend so many secret years in an empty world with one woman. But our Writers deservedly reject this crabbed opinion; and defend that there is a peculiar comfort in the married state besides the genial bed, which no other society affords.[5]

In this passage, Milton elevates companionate marriage above masculine friendship, that affective bond so many Renaissance humanists heralded as superior to heterosocial relations.⁶ Pointing to this and other examples from his polemics and poems, critics have identified Milton's participation in a discernible epistemic shift in the so-called sexual norm: when homonormative friendship was superseded by heteronormative marriage.⁷ According to Gregory Chaplin, "The marital ideal that Milton articulates in his divorce tracts . . . develops out of the Platonically inspired friendship that he shared with Charles Diodati. Milton's theory of marriage thus represents the fusion of two discourses: Christian marriage, as modified by reformed theologians and humanist scholars, and Renaissance friendship – the practice of classical friendship revived by humanist educators and the dissemination of classical texts."⁸ Likewise, Thomas Luxon argues that Milton seeks "to redefine marriage using terms and principles of classical friendship, and then to promote this newly dignified version of marriage as the originary human relation and, therefore, the bedrock of social and political culture in Protestant Christendom."⁹ Milton's project, then, was to appropriate the rhetoric of masculine friendship for companionate marriage.

Without denying the importance of friendship in Milton's ruminations about marriage, I submit that the paradigm put forward by Chaplin, Luxon, and others has had a potentially totalizing effect on Milton criticism. That is, the scholarly emphasis on friendship and marriage – as opposed to a wider range of hetero- and homoerotic relations that defy and exceed these dominant paradigms – has established a false binary. Thus, whereas Chaplin claims that Milton's deployment of Eros and Anteros in *Doctrine* "depict[s] the marital bond because his friendship with Diodati serves as the basis of the marital ideal he develops," I propose that the myth about the erotes posits a dynamic that resists any easy categorization.¹⁰ Examining the version of Eros and Anteros we find in *Doctrine* in the context of the rich tradition from which it emerged, I aim to show that Milton puts into discourse a concept of mutual love separated out from preexisting social structures. I want to argue that Milton exploits the slew of contradictions and controversies attached to the story of Eros and Anteros in order to articulate a hitherto ineffable mutual love – what I am calling "queer mutuality." Not only is this mutuality distinct from institutions such as friendship and marriage; it is also put in the service of exposing the tyranny of those institutions. That Milton would offer a critique of marriage in a chapter that in fact focuses on matrimonial love might seem paradoxical. As I hope to demonstrate, however, this paradox enables the polemicist to distinguish sharply between institutions of friendship and marriage on the one hand and the mutualities they often disallow on the other. In so doing, Milton opens up a conceptual gulf wherein the radical queer potential of his argument might be realized. For even if he could not have anticipated the sexual politics of the modern era, the primacy Milton affords mutual love irrespective of cultural expectations appears strikingly similar to queer critiques of marriage and the neoliberal state.¹¹

The argument of Book One, Chapter 6 in *Doctrine* rehearses, at the same time that it interrogates, the terms and conditions of marriage that most concern Milton: "God regards Love and Peace in the family more than a compulsive performance of marriage, which is more broke by a grievous continuance than by a needful divorce."¹² In this argument, Milton throws into relief crucial differences between marriage, which often requires "compulsive performance" and "grievous continuance," and reciprocal love founded upon "Love and Peace." In the chapter itself, Milton develops this distinction, explaining that marriage and love are not synonymous; on the contrary, in many cases they oppose one another: "this is a deep and serious verity, showing us that love in marriage cannot live nor subsist unless it be mutual; and where love cannot be, there can be left of wedlock nothing but the empty husk of an outside matrimony, as undelightful and unpleasing to God as any other kind of hypocrisy" (711). In fulminating against the "hypocrisy" that confers marital status upon individuals who do not love one another, Milton acknowledges that mutual love differs fundamentally from, and therefore exists independently of, the state of matrimony. Moreover, Milton insists upon the primacy of "love in marriage," without which "wedlock [is] nothing but the empty husk." In other words, what concerns Milton most here is not the integrity of the married state, but rather the threat marriage poses to love's "subsist[ence]."

To elucidate this originary mutual love, Milton provides his own adaptation of the myth of Eros and Anteros. In what might be an attempt to bridge the gap between love and marriage, Milton calls the story a "parabl[e]" of "matrimonial love" (711). However, the tale has nothing to say about the cultivation of love within the constraints of wedlock; it explores, rather, the discovery of mutual love and desire irrespective of any social institutions. Beginning at the end, we note that in Milton's version, when Eros finally encounters his brother Anteros, their union is described as "the reflection of a coequal and homogeneal fire" (711). What kind of love is this, exactly? Though some artists did heterosexualize the myth, depicting Eros and Anteros as a mixed-sex couple (fig. 3), these renditions make up a relatively small portion of Renaissance interpretations. In general, Renaissance artists maintained the homoerotic dynamic of Eros and Anteros's coupling, prompting one to wonder why Milton would choose it as the vehicle for expressing mutual love vis-à-vis marriage. Though one might think that the Neoplatonic reading of the tale appealed to Milton, in the discussion that follows I shall show that the images of tumescence and ejaculation he enlists in his version indicate a resistance to a narrowly allegorical interpretation. It will also become clear, however, that the mutuality Milton illustrates is not necessarily reducible to an erotic encounter. Drawing upon a range of sources that contest and contradict one another, Milton uses Eros and Anteros to articulate a dynamic that remains tantalizingly out of reach, intelligible more for what it isn't – namely, friendship or marriage, or rather friendship or marriage *as such* – than what it is or could be. Or to put it another way, the wide spectrum of possibilities separated out from preexisting social arrangements, friendship and marriage among them, makes Milton's parable of Eros and Anteros so obviously invested in a kind of queer mutuality.

Figure 3: "Requited Love Represented by Eros and Anteros," engraving by Jacob Matham (1588). Digital Image © 2013 Museum Associates / LACMA. Licensed by Art Resource, NY.

In some respects, the tale we find in *Doctrine* is of a piece with Milton's other works emphasizing the need for one to discern right from wrong, good from evil. Eros searches "all about" for his brother Anteros, along the way meeting "many false and feigning desires that wander singly up and down in his likeness" (711). Whose "likeness" the "false and feigning desires" inhabit remains unclear. They might be impersonating Anteros, since he is the one Eros has set out to find. But they might also be disguised as Eros, since Milton, following Themistius, claims that "Love, if he be not twin-born, yet hath a brother wondrous like him, called Anteros" (711).[13] In any event, Eros finds himself in the by-now familiar Miltonic position, tasked with differentiating between true love and "false and feigning desires." In fact, the quest is even more difficult than it first appears. If we accept that Milton knew of and drew upon multiple accounts of the myth, and indeed this is one of my premises, then in addition to finding his brother Anteros, Eros must also locate the correct form of him. Although many Renaissance works identify Anteros as the embodiment of mutual or reciprocal love, in Pausanias's second-century *Description of Greece*, a text Milton would have known, Anteros represents something entirely different – what W.H.S. Jones translates as "love avenged":

> πρὸ δὲ τῆς ἐσόδου τῆς ἐς Ἀκαδημίαν ἐστὶ βωμὸς Ἔρωτος ἔχων ἐπίγραμμα ὡς Χάρμος Ἀθηναίων πρῶτος Ἔρωτι ἀναθείη. τὸν δὲ ἐν πόλει βωμὸν καλούμενον Ἀντέρωτος

ἀνάθημα εἶναι λέγουσι μετοίκων, ὅτι Μέλης Ἀθηναῖος μέτοικον ἄνδρα Τιμαγόραν ἐρασθέντα ἀτιμάζων ἀφεῖναι κατὰ τῆς πέτρας αὐτὸν ἐκέλευσεν ἐς τὸ ὑψηλότατον αὐτῆς ἀνελθόντα· Τιμαγόρας δὲ ἄρα καὶ ψυχῆς εἶχεν ἀφειδῶς καὶ πάντα ὁμοίως κελεύοντι ἤθελε χαρίζεσθαι τῷ μειρακίῳ καὶ δὴ καὶ φέρων ἑαυτὸν ἀφῆκε· Μέλητα δέ, ὡς ἀποθανόντα εἶδε Τιμαγόραν, ἐς τοσοῦτο μετανοίας ἐλθεῖν ὡς πεσεῖν τε ἀπὸ τῆς πέτρας τῆς αὐτῆς καὶ οὕτως ἀφεὶς αὐτὸν ἐτελεύτησε. καὶ τὸ ἐντεῦθεν δαίμονα Ἀντέρωτα τὸν ἀλάστορα τὸν Τιμαγόρου κατέστη τοῖς μετοίκοις νομίζειν.

[Before the entrance to the Academy is an altar to Love, with an inscription that Charmus was the first Athenian to dedicate an altar to that god. The altar within the city called the altar of Anteros they say was dedicated by resident aliens, because the Athenian Meles, spurning the love of Timagoras, a resident alien, bade him ascend to the highest point of the rock and cast himself down. When Meles saw that Timagoras was dead, he suffered such pangs of remorse that he threw himself from the same rock and so died. From this time the resident aliens worshipped as Anteros the avenging spirit of Timagoras.][14]

In this passage, Anteros represents not love returned but love spurned, a love that sends Timagoras and Meles to their deaths. As the avenging spirit of Timagoras, Anteros designs to punish those who scorn love even, perhaps especially, when the lover is a foreigner. I shall have more to say about the tragic trajectory of Pausanias's version of the tale. For now, it should suffice to note that if Milton's parable focuses on the eventual union of the erotes, then this union would entail Eros's finding one instantiation of Anteros while avoiding the wrath of another. Thus, at the same time that he must discern between the "many false and feigning desires" that may appear as Eros and/or Anteros, Eros must also discern between Anteros as Love Returned and Anteros as Love Avenged.

    The misrecognition of love and desire that mobilizes Milton's tale is also of central importance to the earliest depiction of Anteros, which we find in Plato's *Phaedrus*. Though editors of *Doctrine* regularly cite Plato as Milton's chief source, the particulars of the passage in question cast serious doubt on critical interpretations that take masculine friendship as the salient model for Miltonic marriage.[15] Appearing in *Phaedrus* as a concept rather than a cherub, anteros (ἀντέρωτα) names the *physical* desire felt between lover and beloved, erastes and eromenos. In the famous chariot allegory, Socrates explains that each lover is a charioteer, his chariot pulled by two horses:

ὅταν δ' οὖν ὁ ἡνίοχος ἰδὼν τὸ ἐρωτικὸν ὄμμα, πᾶσαν αἰσθήσει διαθερμήνας τὴν ψυχήν, γαργαλισμοῦ τε καὶ πόθου κέντρων ὑποπλησθῇ, ὁ μὲν εὐπειθὴς τῷ ἡνιόχῳ τῶν ἵππων, ἀεί τε καὶ τότε αἰδοῖ βιαζόμενος, ἑαυτὸν κατέχει μὴ ἐπιπηδᾶν τῷ ἐρωμένῳ· ὁ δὲ οὔτε κέντρων ἡνιοχικῶν οὔτε μάστιγος ἔτι ἐντρέπεται, σκιρτῶν δὲ βίᾳ φέρεται, καὶ πάντα πράγματα παρέχων τῷ συζύγι τε καὶ ἡνιόχῳ ἀναγκάζει ἰέναι τε πρὸς τὰ παιδικὰ καὶ μνείαν ποιεῖσθαι τῆς τῶν ἀφροδισίων χάριτος.

[Now when the charioteer beholds the love-inspiring vision, and his whole soul is warmed by the sight, and is full of the tickling and prickings of yearning, the horse that is obedient the charioteer, constrained then as always by modesty, controls himself and does not leap upon the beloved; but the other no longer heeds the pricks or the whip of the charioteer, but springs wildly forward, causing all possible trouble to his mate and to the charioteer, and forcing them to approach the beloved and propose the joys of love.][16]

Although Socrates warns against allowing the concupiscent horse to drive the chariot, his description of reciprocal love suggests that such consummation is not just desirable but often inevitable:

ἐρᾷ μὲν οὖν, ὅτου δὲ ἀπορεῖ· καὶ οὔθ' ὅτι πέπονθεν οἶδεν οὐδ' ἔχει φράσαι, ἀλλ' οἷον ἀπ' ἄλλου ὀφθαλμίας ἀπολελαυκὼς πρόφασιν εἰπεῖν οὐκ ἔχει, ὥσπερ δὲ ἐν κατόπτρῳ ἐν τῷ ἐρῶντι ἑαυτὸν ὁρῶν λέληθεν. καὶ ὅταν μὲν ἐκεῖνος παρῇ, λήγει κατὰ ταὐτὰ ἐκείνῳ τῆς ὀδύνης, ὅταν δὲ ἀπῇ, κατὰ ταὐτὰ αὖ ποθεῖ καὶ ποθεῖται, εἴδωλον ἔρωτος ἀντέρωτα ἔχων· καλεῖ δὲ αὐτὸν καὶ οἴεται οὐκ ἔρωτα ἀλλὰ φιλίαν εἶναι. ἐπιθυμεῖ δὲ ἐκείνῳ παραπλησίως μέν, ἀσθενεστέρως δέ, ὁρᾶν, ἅπτεσθαι, φιλεῖν, συγκατακεῖσθαι· καὶ δή, οἷον εἰκός, ποιεῖ τὸ μετὰ τοῦτο ταχὺ ταῦτα.

[So he is in love, but he knows not with whom; he does not understand his own condition and cannot explain it; like one who has caught a disease of the eyes from another, he can give no reason for it; he sees himself in his lover as in a mirror, but is not conscious of the fact. And in the lover's presence, like him he ceases from his pain, and in his absence, like him he is filled with yearning such as he inspires, and love's image, requited love, dwells within him; but he calls it, and believes it to be, not love, but friendship. Like the lover, though less strongly, he desires to see his friend, to touch him, kiss him, and lie down by him; and naturally these things are soon brought about.][17]

In this depiction, anteros signifies a reciprocal or requited love expressed through physical intimacy. Although the critical tendency has been to identify this love as amity, as in Chaplin's reading of Milton's use of *Phaedrus*, Socrates insists, following Harold Fowler's translation, that the lover "*calls it*, and *believes it to be*, not love, but friendship." This distinction is crucial: not only does Socrates, and through him Plato, distinguish between love (ἔρωτα) and friendship (φιλίαν); he also declares that mutual love is often misrecognized as friendship. More simply put, anteros feels like friendship, when in fact it is something else. This something else, moreover, involves a physical consummation that, propelled by the concupiscent horse, remains distinct from, but not incompatible with, the spiritual love Socrates celebrates as divine madness.

During the Renaissance, at least two interpretations of this consummation became prominent: some humanists sought to de-eroticize the myth, repackaging it as an allegory for choosing spiritual love over carnal love, while others either eschewed this prudish reading altogether or reproduced it so as to lay bare its pretentiousness. If the Shaftesbury Memorial represents a more recent attempt at the former interpretation, Andrea Alciati's *Emblemata* includes a considerably more influential example, one Milton certainly knew. In Emblem CX ("Ἀντέρως, id est, Amor virtutis"), Alciati presents Anteros as "love of virtue":

> Dic ubi sunt incurvi arcus? ubi tela Cupido?
>   Mollia queis iuvenum figere corda soles.
> Fax ubi tristis? ubi pennae? tres unde corollas
>   Fert manus? unde aliam tempora cincta gerunt?
> Haud mihi vulgari est hospes cum Cypride quicquam,
>   Ulla voluptatis nos neque forma tulit.
> Sed puris hominum succendo mentibus ignes
>   Disciplinae, animos astraque ad alta traho.
> Quatuor ecque ipsa texo virtute corollas:
>   Quarum, quae Sophiae est, tempora prima tegit.

["Tell me, where are your arching bows, where your arrows, Cupid, the shafts which you use to pierce the tender hearts of the young? Where is your hurtful torch, where your wings? Why does your hand hold three garlands? Why do your temples wear a fourth? - Stranger, I have nothing to do with common Venus, nor did any pleasurable shape bring me forth. I light the fires of learning in the pure minds of men and draw their thoughts to the stars on high. I weave four garlands out of virtue's self and the chief of these, the garland of Wisdom, wreathes my temples."][18]

The image for this emblem (fig. 4) show Anteros (or is it Eros?) holding a palm, a reference to yet another version of the myth from antiquity. In a different section of his *Description of Greece*, Pausanias observes, ἔστι δὲ καὶ τρίτος γυμνασίου περίβολος, ὄνομα μὲν Μαλθὼ τῆς μαλακότητος τοῦ ἐδάφους ἕνεκα, τοῖς δὲ ἐφήβοις ἀνεῖται τῆς πανηγύρεως τὸν χρόνον πάντα. ἔστι δὲ ἐν γωνίᾳ τῆς Μαλθοῦς πρόσωπον Ἡρακλέους ἄχρι ἐς τοὺς ὤμους, καὶ ἐν τῶν παλαιστρῶν μιᾷ τύπος Ἔρωτα ἔχων ἐπειργασμένον καὶ τὸν καλούμενον Ἀντέρωτα: ἔχει δὲ ὁ μὲν φοίνικος ὁ Ἔρως κλάδον, ὁ δὲ ἀφελέσθαι πειρᾶται τὸν φοίνικα ὁ Ἀντέρως.

[There is also a third enclosed gymnasium, called Maltho from the softness of its floor, and reserved for the youths for the whole time of the festival. In a corner of the Maltho is a bust of Heracles as far as the shoulders, and in one of the wrestling-schools is a relief showing Love and Love Returned, as he is called. Love holds a palm-branch, and Love Returned is trying to take the palm from him.][19]

As Guy de Tervarent has shown, this depiction of Eros and Anteros as competing over a palm was common in Renaissance art.[20] For Neoplatonists such as Alciati, the struggle between Eros and Anteros amounts to a struggle between physical love and spiritual love. That the brothers wrestling for the palm often look identical to one another (figs. 2 and 5) underscores the difficulty of the struggle; they are evenly matched, and more often than not Renaissance artists illustrate not a decisive victory but an ongoing struggle. The twinning of Eros and Anteros also raises questions about the supposed differences between the two kinds of love they embody. Indeed, how do we know Eros from Anteros? And how do we move away, finally, from the eroticized images through which erotic and spiritual love are conveyed?[21] Once again, we find the tenor unable to efface the vehicle. To illustrate the dilemma, one might glance at the text of Emblem CXI from Alciati's *Emblemata*:

> Aligerum, aligeroque inimicum pinxit Amori,
>   Arcu arcum, atque ignes igne domans Nemesis.
> Ut quae aliis fecit, patiatur: at hic puer olim
>   Intrepidus gestans tela, miser lacrimat.
> Ter spuit inque sinus imos: res mira, crematur
>   Igne ignis, furias odit Amoris Amor.

[Nemesis has fashioned a form with wings, a foe to Love with his wings, subduing bow with bow and flames with flame, so that Love may suffer what he has done to others. But this boy, once so bold when he was carrying his arrows, now weeps in misery and has spat three times low on his breast. A wondrous thing - fire is being burned with fire, Love is loathing the frenzies of Love.][22]

On its face, this emblem records Anteros's triumph over Eros, but in the scene Alciati narrates Eros has his carnal desires turned against him, implying that Anteros vanquishes his brother only by outmatching him in the arena of erotic prowess. Here the twinning of Eros and Anteros confounds the very qualities Alciati is at such pains to differentiate.

Figure 4: Emblem CX, from Andrea Alciati, *Emblemata cum commentariis Claudii Minois I.C. Francisci Sanctii Brocensis, & notis Laurentii Pignarii Patavini* . . . Opera et vigiliis Ioannis Accesserunt in fine Federici Morelli Professoris Regij (Padua, 1621), 457.

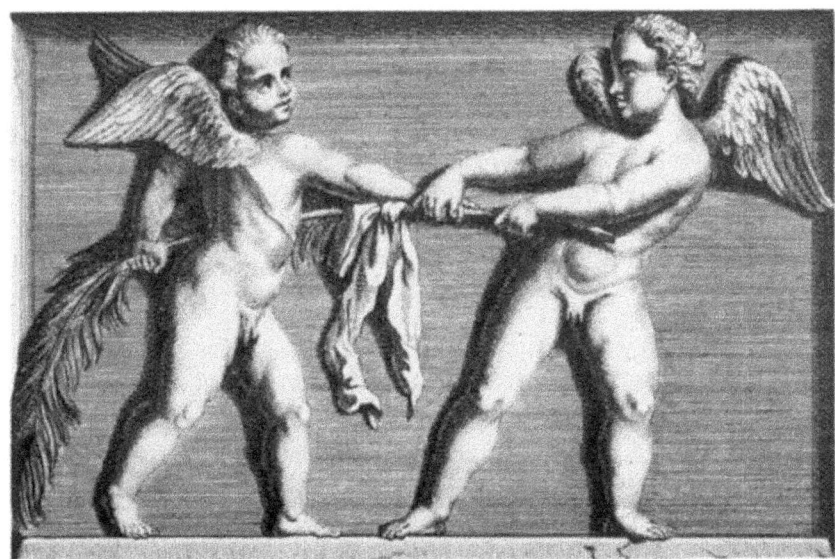
Figure 5: Engraving of Eros and Anteros wrestling over the palm, from Bernard de Montfaucon, *Antiquity explained, and represented in sculptures*, trans. David Humphreys, Vol. 1 (London, 1721), 117.

If Alciati allies himself with the Neoplatonists, Milton, in rejecting a narrowly allegorical view of Eros and Anteros, gravitates more towards Plato and the dialogue on love as divine madness in *Phaedrus*. So, too, does Ben Jonson, whom Merritt Hughes cites as a contemporary source for Milton's representation of the erotes.[23] Before attending to the homoerotics of the excerpt from *Doctrine*, then, I would like to turn briefly to one of Jonson's masques that appears to have been formative for Milton. Performed at Bolsover Castle in 1634 and printed in 1641, *Love's Welcome* was likely Jonson's final court masque. Staged in honor of King Charles I and Queen Henrietta Maria, the masque begins with the chorus's pondering the nature of love:

Chor.	If LOVE be call'd a lifting of the Sense,
	To knowledge of that pure intelligence,
	Wherein the Soule hath rest, and residence;
1 Tenor	When were the Senses in such order plac'd?
2 Tenor	The Sight, the Hearing, Smelling, Touching, Taste,
	All at one banquet?
Base	'Would it ever last![24]

Though the meditation begins with the Neoclasically informed idea that love must transcend "Sense, / To knowledge of that pure intelligence," the individual voices that make up the chorus go on to undermine such a view by conceiving of love as a sensual banquet. The masque's stage directions indicate that an actual banquet is then set before the king and queen, but not before the chorus concludes, "And hence, / At every reall banquet to the Sense, / Welcome, true Welcome fill the Complements" (808). Although the interactive aspect of the performance is de rigueur for Stuart masques, this particular gesture conscripts into a polyamorous feast of love not just the sovereign and his queen but everyone in attendance.

One might suspect that this initial feast belongs to the Jonsonian antimasque, the place where chaos and discord are simulated. However, Eros and Anteros's introduction into the masque's interrogation of love suggests that Neoplatonic ascent is finally not possible. Nor is it desirable. Jonson's skepticism is evident in the stage directions that describe the first entrance of Eros and Anteros:

> And the King, and Queene, having a second Banquet set downe before them from the Cloudes by two Loves; One, as the Kings, with a bough of Palme (in his hand) cleft a little at the top, the other as the Queenes; differenced by their Garlands only: His of White, and Red Roses; the other of Lilly's inter-weav'd, Gold, Silver, Purple, &c. They were both arm'd, and wing'd: with Bowes and Quivers, Cassocks, Breeches, Buskins, Gloves, and Perukes alike. They stood silent awhile, wondring at one another, till at last the lesser of them began to speake. (810)

Here, as elsewhere, Eros and Anteros remain virtually indistinguishable, the only marker of difference the color of their garlands. In fact, they look so similar that their entrance is punctuated by an awkward silence as they "wond[er] at one another." At this moment, Jonson affords spectators the ability to see the embodiment of Eros and Anteros as a process that culminates in their becoming aware of one another's existence. As usual, the erotes wrestle over the palm, but whereas Renaissance artists tend to depict the struggle rather than the outcome, and whereas Neoplatonists tend to insist that of course Anteros wins, Jonson's stage directions indicate that "Anteros snatch'd at the Palme, but Eros divided it" (811). In addition to giving Eros rather than Anteros agency in this situation, Jonson allows that Eros might make the rational decision to split the palm between the two brothers. Indeed, if either of the brothers is to be labeled irrational, it is the overzealous and uncompromising Anteros seen "snatch[ing] at the Palme." As for the act itself, Eros's dividing the palm exemplifies a palpable shift away from Neoplatonism and back toward Plato. As in Socrates' chariot allegory in *Phaedrus*, erotic love and spiritual love are not found to be mutually exclusive – or at least not inherently so. Although Jonson's revision of the palm incident might seem minor, it can be read as a rebuke of the unrealistic, even undesirable views of Neoplatonists who, like Anteros and Alciati, think Eros has no claim to the palm in the first place.[25]

The palm's division might serve as a diplomatic resolution to the argument between cherubs, but Eros and Anteros at peace are no less disruptive to the masque's representation of love, since any admission of carnality between the brothers activates and brings to the fore the latent homoeroticism of this dynamic. Indeed, moments later the reconciled erotes return to expound on mutual love, an exchange that will get them booted from the performance:

Eros	We ha' cleft the bough,
	And struck a tallie of our loves, too, now.
Anteros	I call to mind the wisdome of our Mother,
	Venus, who would have Cupid have a Brother-
Eros	To looke upon, and thrive. Mee seemes I grew
	Three inches higher sin' I met with you.
Anteros	It was the Counsell, that the Oracle gave
	Your Nurses, the glad Graces, sent to crave
	Themis advice. You doe not know (quoth shee)
	The nature of this Infant. Love may be
	Brought forth thus little, live, a-while, alone;
	But ne're will prosper, if he have not one
	Sent after him to play with.
Eros	Such another
	As you are, Anteros, our loving brother.
Anteros	Who would be, always, planted in your eye;
	For Love, by Love, increaseth mutually.
Eros	Wee, either, looking on each other, thrive;
Anteros	Shoot up, grow galliard –
Eros	Yes, and more alive!
Anteros	When one's away, it seemes we both are lesse.
Eros	I was a Dwarfe, an Urchin, I confesse,
	Till you were present. (811-812)

Throughout the dialogue, Eros and Anteros express mutual love through the image of tumescence.[26] As they begin to experience reciprocal love, Eros becomes aroused, declaring that he "grew / Three inches higher sin' [he] met with" Anteros. For his part, Anteros encourages his brother to grow even bigger – to "Shoot up, grow galliard." Here reciprocal love acts as an aphrodisiac, enhancing erotic desire. As the flirtation continues, the dialogue becomes stichomythic, enacting the rhythms of intercourse. In the unlikely event that some onlookers have missed the bawdiness of the encounter, Philalethes enters to prevent the erotes from carrying things too far: "No more of your Poetrie (prettie Cupids) lest presuming on your little wits, you prophane the intention of your service" (812). Philalethes does not clarify whether homoerotic acts in themselves or their performance before the king and queen threaten to "prophane the intention" of Eros and Anteros. Either way, the exchange makes explicit that the mutuality embodied in Jonson's Eros and Anteros is not the transcendent love of the Neoplatonists.

In the masque's final monologue, Philalethes attempts to reconcile the love exemplified in Eros and Anteros with the strictures of marriage, but the result suggests a fundamental disconnection between the two. That is, while mutual love and marriage are not necessarily diametrically opposed, they are not synonymous either. After scolding the erotes, Philalethes calls the court a "School-Divinitie of Love" and informs them, "Here you shall read Hymen, having lighted two Torches, either of which enflame mutually, but waste not. One Love by the others aspect increasing, and both in right lines aspiring" (813). Though Philalethes endeavors to bend the erotes' desires toward marriage, the language of tumescence returns in his forecasting that the boys will "increase" and "inspire." What is more, the need for a "School-Divinitie of Love" where the erotes will be taught how to abide marital obligations implies that while mutual love is natural, matrimonial love is cultural.[27] Although Eros and Anteros, no less than Adam and Eve, are, as Jonson's dialogue shows, companions fashioned for one another, the erotes radically oppose, even as they resemble, Biblically sanctioned matrimonial love.[28]

The similarities between Milton's and Jonson's representations of Eros and Anteros indicate that the authors had comparable views on the kind of love the erotes signify. Like Jonson, Milton rejects a purely allegorical reading of the story. Also like Jonson, Milton invokes tumescence to illustrate Eros's discovering Anteros:

> [S]traight his arrows lose their golden heads and shed their purple feathers, his silken braids untwine and slip their knots, and that original and fiery virtue given him by fate all on a sudden goes out, and leave him undeified and despoiled of all his force; till finding Anteros at last, he kindles and repairs the almost faded ammunition of his deity by the reflection of a coequal and homogeneal fire. (711)

Desperate to cast off the "many false and feigning desires that wander singly up and down in his likeness" and find his brother Anteros, Eros grows flaccid. The arrows representing his phallic power "lose their golden heads and shed their purple feathers," while the "silken braids" that evidence his potency "untwine." Upon finding Anteros, he "kindles and repairs the almost faded ammunition," regaining his phallic "force." As in Jonson's masque, the coupling of Eros and Anteros evinces a consummated homoerotic love that an allegorical reading cannot finally contain. On this point, it bears notice that Milton, following Jonson, does not award Anteros victory over Eros. On the contrary, Eros and Anteros merge in "a coequal and homogeneal fire." This union may recall the Biblical account of the married couple's becoming "one flesh," but for Milton the "coequal and homogeneal fire" of mutual love *precedes* marriage.[29] Hence, while Jane Kingsley-Smith has argued that by the close of the seventeenth century, Cupid, especially as he is portrayed in masques, suffers from a "dematerialization of eros," thereby "los[ing] power and agency," in Jonson's and Milton's renderings, the erotes' phallic abilities are enhanced rather than depleted.[30]

Moreover, the erotes' coming together in "a coequal and homogeneal fire" points to a relationship that exists apart from, perhaps even in contradistinction to, dominant cultural institutions. Founded upon sameness, the bond of Eros and Anteros exhibits a homogeneity that seems closer to the angelic relations Stephen Guy-Bray examines in his essay for this special issue than the union of husband and wife. Thus, the originary "coequal and homogeneal fire" of the erotes remains distinct from the "matrimonial love" Milton mentions at the beginning of Book One, Chapter 6 in *Doctrine*. Although the one should, in Milton's view, lead to the other, the need for divorce implies that often such is not the case. But if mutual love does not equal marriage, neither does it fall under the rubric of amicitia. As the excerpt from *Phaedrus* reminds us, Anteros stands for a love mistaken for friendship. With Eros and Anteros, then, Milton articulates an originary mutual love that becomes legible through a consideration of what it isn't. In distinguishing this mutuality from marriage and friendship, Milton posits a queer dynamic that resists absorption into preexisting relationalities. Although for Milton this mutuality is phallicly constituted, figured in images of tumescence and male ejaculation, the emphasis on homogeneity in Eros and Anteros's consummation of their love does, I think, create a space for female homoerotic desire. That is, while Milton uses a story of male homoerotic desire to envisage a mutuality that cannot be subsumed under discourses of friendship or marriage, the implications for this parable extend to any couple whose love defies normalizing institutions such as friendship or marriage.

To make sense of Milton's understanding of mutual love as both requisite for and potentially incompatible with matrimony and matrimonial love, one might consider the tragic events that underlie a number of classical stories delineating Anteros's origins. In the passage from Pausanias's *Description of Greece* I quoted earlier, Anteros personifies Love Avenged. This version comes into existence when the Athenian Meles spurns the love of a resident alien named Timagoras. Upon seeing Timagoras's corpse, Meles felt such insurmountable remorse that, in the words of Jones's translation, "he threw himself from the same rock and so died." According to this version of the story, Love Avenged emerges from the unrequited love of one man for another. That Pausanias notes the different nationalities of Meles and Timagoras suggests that xenophobia rather than homophobia is the motivating factor for the rejection, but here, as in other versions of the tale, one could read this incident as one of misrecognition, one that proves fatal. Only after Timagoras has done as his would-be lover has ordered does Meles realize the egregious mistake he has made. And so, in an act that reflects his acknowledgment of and atonement for the error he has committed, Meles joins in his lover in death.

One of Pausanias's contemporaries, Aelian, traces a different etiology of Anteros in *On the Characteristics of Animals*. Although Anteros is manifest in the requited love of Poseiden and Nerites, a same-sex relationship that is also intergenerational, it, too, ends in tragedy:

> ὁ δὲ ἄλλος λόγος ἐρασθῆναι βοᾷ Νηρίτου Ποσειδῶνα, ἀντερᾶν δὲ τοῦ Ποσειδῶνος, καὶ τοῦ γε ὑμνουμένου Ἀντέρωτος ἐντεῦθεν τὴν γένεσιν ὑπάρξασθαι. συνδιατρίβειν οὖν τά τε ἄλλα τῷ ἐραστῇ τὸν ἐρώμενον ἀκούω καὶ μέντοι καὶ αὐτοῦ ἐλαύνοντος κατὰ τῶν κυμάτων τὸ ἅρμα τὰ μὲν κήτη τἄλλα καὶ τοὺς δελφῖνας καὶ προσέτι καὶ τοὺς Τρίτωνας ἀναπηδᾶν ἐκ τῶν μυχῶν καὶ περισκιρτᾶν τὸ ἅρμα καὶ

περιχορεύειν, ἀπολείπεσθαι δ᾽ οὖν τοῦ τάχους τῶν ἵππων πάντως καὶ πάντῃ: μόνα δὲ ἄρα τὰ παιδικὰ οἱ παρομαρτεῖν καὶ μάλα πλησίον, στορνυσθαι δὲ αὐτοῖς καὶ τὸ κῦμα καὶ διίστασθαι τὴν θάλατταν αἰδοῖ Ποσειδῶνος: βούλεσθαι γὰρ τῇ τε ἄλλῃ τὸν θεὸν εὐδοκιμεῖν τὸν καλὸν ἐρώμενον καὶ οὖν καὶ τῇ νήξει διαπρέπειν.

[But the other account proclaims that Poseiden was the lover of Nerites, and that Nerites returned his love, and that this was the origin of celebrated Anteros. And so, as I am told, for the favourite spent his time with his lover, and moreover when Poseidon drove his chariot over the waves, all other great fishes as well as dolphins and tritons too, sprang up from their deep haunts and gambolled and danced around the chariot, only to be left utterly and far behind by the speed of his horses; only the boy favourite was his escort close at hand, and before them the waves sank to rest and the sea parted out of reverence to Poseidon, for the god willed that his beautiful favourite should not only be highly esteemed for other reasons but should also be pre-eminent at swimming.][31]

All is well until Apollo, in the form of the Sun, transforms Nerites into a spiral shell. At first Aelian proposes that Apollo metamorphoses the boy on account of his quickness, but it soon becomes clear that this explanation is merely a pretense:

τὸν δὲ Ἥλιον νεμεσῆσαι τῷ τάχει τοῦ παιδὸς ὁ μῦθος λέγει, καὶ ἀμεῖψαί οἱ τὸ σῶμα ἐς τὸν κόχλον τὸν νῦν, οὐκ οἶδα εἰπεῖν ὁπόθεν ἀγριάναντα: οὐδὲ γὰρ ὁ μῦθος λέγει. εἰ δέ τι χρὴ συμβαλεῖν ὑπὲρ τῶν ἀτεκμάρτων, λέγοιντ᾽ ἂν ἀντερᾶν Ποσειδῶν καὶ Ἥλιος. καὶ ἠγανάκτει μὲν ἴσως ὁ Ἥλιος ὡς ἐν θαλάττῃ φερομένῳ, ἐβούλετο δὲ αὐτὸν οὐκ ἐν τοῖς κήτεσιν ἀριθμεῖσθαι, ἀλλ᾽ ἐν ἄστροις φέρεσθαι.

[But the story relates that the Sun resented the boy's power of speed and transformed his body into the spiral shell as it now is: the cause of his anger I cannot tell, neither does the fable mention it. But if one may guess where there is nothing to go by, Poseidon and the Sun might be said to be rivals. And it may be that the Sun was vexed at the boy travelling about the sea and wished that he should travel among the constellations instead of being counted among sea-monsters.][32]

Though Aelian locates the origin of Anteros in Poseiden and Nerites' love for one another, the tragedy that befalls the intergenerational same-sex couple suggests that this love is elegiac, consigned to the past. In this instance, Anteros comes closest to occupying that paradoxical position where he inhabits both Love Returned and Love Avenged, since the requited love Poseidon and Nerites share is destroyed by a god jealous of their relationship.

Aelian's story is also notable for its juxtaposing reciprocal love, which is homoerotic and tragic, with marriage, which is heteroerotic and procreative. Or to borrow Lee Edelman's popular phrase, we could say that Aelian's tale suggests that the love Anteros symbolizes has "no future."[33] Indeed, Poseidon and Apollo, the gods vying over Nerites, are veteran pederasts: in addition to loving Nerites, Poseidon loves Pelops (and Ganymede, according to Marlowe's *Hero and Leander*); Apollo, meanwhile, also loves Hyacinthus. These instances of mutual love are also short-lived: Pelops goes on to marry, have children, and found royal dynasties of Greece, while Hyacinthus is killed by a wayward discuss and subsequently metamorphosed into a flower.[34] According to Aelian, then, mutual love is not only homoerotic and intergenerational but also elegiac, destined to end either in marriage or in death.

One could argue that the tragic trajectories of Pausanias and Aelian help explain the gap Milton opens up between mutual love and marriage in *Doctrine*, but I want to resist the temptation to oversimplify the matter and add this text to the massive heap of works associating homoerotic desire with death. Returning Eros and Anteros to their immediate Miltonic context, we are reminded that the polemicist is employing the allusion to make a point about the disconnection between mutual love and marriage. And as Milton makes clear throughout his divorce tracts, mutual love is not the problem. In the final sentence of the chapter that features Eros and Anteros, Milton concludes,

> And it is a less breach of wedlock to part with wise and quiet consent betimes, than still to soil and profane that mystery of joy and union with a polluting sadness and perpetual distemper: for it is not the outward continuing of marriage that keeps whole that covenant, but whosoever does most according to peace and love, whether in marriage or in divorce, he it is that breaks marriage least; it being so often written, that "Love only is the fulfilling of every commandment." (712)

As one of his contemporaries was quick to point out, Milton's quotation of Romans contains a subtle yet potentially radical modification: whereas Paul writes, "Love is the fulfilling of every Commandment," Milton declares, "Love *only* is the fulfilling of every commandment."[35] Milton's insistence that "Love only" matters in "keep[ing] whole that covenant" subordinates marriage to the sustaining love I have been calling "queer mutuality." Appealing to the tragic elements of Anteros in order to suggest the disastrous effects matrimony has had on this mutual love – indeed, on all "coequal and homogeneal fire[s]," in all their permutations –

Milton transforms the love of Anteros into the divine's imperative for humanity. Sometimes divorce is the *only* way to keep God's commandments.

How exactly divorce might sustain this queer love (one would presume it signals its end) is one question Milton's argument raises but does not answer. Nevertheless, in the process of bemoaning marriage's tyranny over those compelled to wed, Milton acknowledges the possibility for what we might call a queer emancipatory politics of love. Of course, the queer politics I perceive in one chapter of one divorce tract do not make Milton a forebear of modern queer movements critical of marriage as a heteronormative, patriarchal institution. Nor do they reflect Milton's clear and final say on matters of love and marriage. As I have shown, Milton's "say" is unclear even in this one divorce tract, to say nothing of his other works.[36] Because I am not convinced, as some critics are, that it is possible to show "how Milton works," or indeed *that* Milton works – at least when "works" amounts to an achievement of argumentative clarity and internal consistency – I view the confused deployment of Eros and Anteros in *Doctrine* as a glimpse into Milton's queer potential for theorizing and politicizing forms of love that do not consolidate into those supported by already existing, normalizing institutions.[37] This potential may not make Milton our contemporary, but it does bring into focus a Milton who takes aim at the same monolithic institutions that preoccupy much queer criticism today.

Notes

1. Quoted in Richard Dorment, "Alfred Gilbert: Biography and Entries," in *Victorian High Renaissance*, by Richard Dorment, Gregory Hedburg, Leonee Ormond, Richard Ormond, and Allen Staley (Minneapolis: Minneapolis Institute of Arts, 1978), 181. In *Anteros: A Forgotten Myth* (London: Routledge, 2011), Craig E. Stephenson reads the sculpture biographically, arguing that Gilbert "associated 'Eros' . . . with the impetuous passion of his younger self and 'Anteros' with a kindly love and selflessness with which he did not easily identify" (68).

2. On the controversies surrounding the construction and erection of the Shaftesbury Memorial, see Stephenson, *Anteros*, 61-75; Jason Edwards, *Alfred Gilbert's Aestheticism: Gilbert Amongst Whistler, Wilde, Leighton, Pater And Burne-Jones* (Aldershot: Ashgate, 2006), 93-132; and Alex Potts, "*Eros* in Piccadilly Circus: Monument and Anti-Monument," in *Sculpture and the Pursuit of a Modern Ideal in Britain c. 1880-1930*, edited by David Getsy (Aldershot: Ashgate, 2004), 105-40.

3. The most comprehensive study of classical, medieval, and Renaissance representations of Eros and Anteros remains Robert V. Merrill, "Eros and Anteros," *Speculum* 19, no. 3 (July 1944): 264-84.

4. Michel Foucault, *The History of Sexuality, Vol 1.: An Introduction*, trans. Robert Hurley (New York: Vintage, 1990), 101.

5. John Milton, *Tetrachordon*, in *Complete Prose Works of Milton, Volume II, 1643-1648*, edited by Ernest Sirluck (New Haven, CT: Yale University Press; London: Oxford University Press, 1959), 596. Milton makes similar point in *Colasterion*, in *Complete Prose Works of Milton, Volume II, 1643-1648*, edited by Ernest Sirluck (New Haven, CT: Yale University Press; London: Oxford University Press, 1959), 739-4

6. On masculine friendship and Renaissance homonormativity, see Laurie Shannon, *Sovereign Amity: Figures of Friendship in Shakespearean Contexts* (Chicago and London: University of Chicago Press, 2002). On challenges to this version of friendship, see Thomas MacFaul, *Male*

Friendship in Shakespeare and his Comedies (Cambridge: Cambridge University Press, 2007), and the essays collected in Daniel T. Lochman, Maritere López, and Lorna Hutson, ed., *Discourses and Representations of Friendship in Early Modern Europe, 1500-1700* (Aldershot: Ashgate, 2011).

7. On the problems with ascribing normative status to any early modern institution, see Karma Lochrie, *Heterosyncrasies: Female Sexuality When Normal Wasn't* (Minneapolis: University of Minnesota Press, 2005).

8. Gregory Chaplin, "'One Flesh, One Heart, One Soul': Renaissance Friendship and Miltonic Marriage," *Modern Philology* 99, no. 2 (November 2001): 266-92; 267.

9. Thomas H. Luxon, *Single Imperfection: Milton, Marriage and Friendship* (Pittsburgh, PA: Duquesne University Press, 2005), 1-2.

10. Chaplin, "Renaissance Friendship and Miltonic Marriage," 283. Other critics who have weighed in on the significance of Milton's friendship with Diodati include John P. Rumrich, "The Erotic Milton," *Texas Studies in Literature and Language* 41, no. 2 (Summer 1999): 128-41; and John T. Shawcross, *John Milton: The Self and the World* (Lexington: the University of Kentucky Press, 2001), esp. ch. 3.

11. For queer critiques of gay marriage movements, see Judith Butler, *Undoing Gender* (New York and London: Routledge, 2004), 102-30; Lisa Duggan, *The Twilight of Equality? Neoliberalism, Cultural Politics, and the Attack on Democracy* (Boston, MA: Beacon Press, 2003), 43-66; Michael Warner, *The Trouble With Normal: Sex, Politics, and the Ethics of Queer Life* (Cambridge, MA: Harvard University Press, 2000), 81-148.

12. John Milton, *Doctrine and Discipline of Divorce*, in *Complete Poems and Major Prose*, edited by Merritt Y. Hughes (Upper Saddle River, NJ: Prentice Hall, 1957), 711. Citations hereafter provided in text.

13. See Oration 24 in Themistius, *The Private Orations of Themistius*, trans. and ed. Robert J. Penella (Berkeley and Los Angeles: University of California Press, 2000), 128-37.

14. Pausanias, *Description of Greece*, Vol. 1, trans. and ed. W.H.S. Jones (Cambridge, MA: Harvard University Press; London: William Heinemann Ltd, 1969), 1.30.1.

15. For a few examples of the critical tendency to cite *Phaedrus* as Milton's primary source, see Merritt Hughes, ed., *Complete Poems and Major Prose* (Indianapolis, IN: Hackett, 2003), 711; Ernest Sirluck, ed., *Complete Prose Works of Milton, Volume II, 1643-1648* (New Haven, CT: Yale University Press; London: Oxford University Press, 1959), 254-55; and Sara J. van den Berg and W. Scott Howard, ed., *The Divorce Contracts of John Milton: Texts and Contexts* (Pittsburgh, PA: Duquesne University Press, 2010), 465.

16. Plato, *Phaedrus*, in *Plato: Euthyphro, Apology, Crito, Phaedo, Phaedrus*, trans. and ed. Harold North Fowler (Cambridge, MA, and London: Harvard University Press, 1999), 253e-254a.

17. Ibid., 255d-255e.

18. Andrea Alciati, *Emblemata cum commentariis Claudii Minois I.C. Francisci Sanctii Brocensis, & notis Laurentii Pignarii Patavini . . . Opera et vigiliis Ioannis Accesserunt in fine Federici Morelli Professoris Regij* (Padua, 1621), p. 457. I have modernized "u/v" in my transcription. The English translation is from "Alciato at Glasgow," Glasgow University Emblem Website, http://www.emblems.arts.gla.ac.uk/alciato/emblem.php?id=A21a110.

19. Pausanias, *Description of Greece*, Vol. 3, trans. and ed. W.H.S. Jones (Cambridge, MA: Harvard University Press; London: William Heinemann Ltd, 1966), 6.23.5.

20. Guy de Tervarent, "Eros and Anteros or Reciprocal Love in Ancient and Renaissance Art," *Journal of the Warburg and Courtauld Institutes* 28 (1965): 205-208.

21. On Shakespeare's pursuit of these questions, see Peggy Munoz Simonds, "Eros and Anteros in Shakespeare's Sonnets 153 and 154: An Iconographical Study," *Spenser Studies* 7 (1987): 261-86.

22. Alciati, *Emblemata cum commentariis*, 461-62. English translation from "Alciato at Glasgow," http://www.emblems.arts.gla.ac.uk/alciato/emblem.php?id=A21a111.

23. Hughes, *Complete Poems and Major Prose*, 711. Hughes mentions a poem titled *Eros and Anteros*, but I have not been able to locate any work bearing this title. I have, however, found at least four works by Jonson that include Eros and Anteros: *Challenge at Tilt, Cynthia's Revels, Love Restored*, and *Love's Welcome at Bolsover*.

24. Jonson, *Love's Welcome at Bolsover*, 807. Citations hereafter provided in text.

25. On the antimasque/masque structure, see Stephen Orgel, *The Jonsonian Masque* (New York: Columbia University Press, 1981). Cf. Lesley Mickel, *Ben Jonson's Antimasques: A History of Growth and Decline* (Aldershot: Ashgate, 1999).

26. Apparently, Jonson was more than a little intrigued by Eros and Anteros's penises. He makes a similar connection between tumescence and Eros and Anteros's love in another masque, *Challenge at Tilt*. See David Riggs, *Ben Jonson: A Life* (Cambridge, MA: Harvard University Press, 1989), 202-203.

27. For an incisive reading of homoerotic love as preceding and less a cultural construct than heteroerotic love and marriage, see Stephen Guy-Bray, "Shakespeare and the Invention of the Heterosexual," *Early Modern Literary Studies* Special Issue 16 (October 2007): 12.1-28 http://purl.oclc.org/emls/si-16/brayshks.htm.

28. *Geneva Bible*, Gen. 2:20.

29. *Geneva Bible*, Gen. 2.24, Mark 10.8.

30. Jane Kingsley-Smith, *Cupid in Early Modern Literature and Culture* (Cambridge: Cambridge University Press, 2010), 177.

31. Aelian, *On the Characteristics of Animals*, Vol. 3, trans. A.F. Schofield, Loeb Classical Library (London: William Heinemann Ltd; Cambridge, MA: Harvard University Press, 1959), 14.28.

32. Ibid.

33. Lee Edelman, *No Future: Queer Theory and the Death Drive* (Durham, NC, and London: Duke University Press, 2004).

34. On Poseidon's love for Pelops, see Pindar, *First Olympian Ode*, in *"Olympian Odes" and "Pythian Odes,"* trans. and ed. William H. Race (Cambridge, MA, and London: Harvard University Press, 1997), 71; on his love for Ganymede, see Marlowe, *Hero and Leander*, in *The Collected Poems of Christopher Marlowe*, ed. Patrick Cheney and Brian J. Striar (Oxford: Oxford University Press, 2005), 639-712; on Apollo's love for Hyacinthus, see Apollodorus, *The Library of Greek Mythology*, trans. and ed. Robin Hard (Oxford: Oxford University Press, 2008), 1.3.3.

35. Anon., *An Answer to a book intituled, The doctrine and discipline of divorce* (London, 1644), 37. The passage in dispute is Romans 13:10.

36. On Milton's inconsistency across his corpus, see Peter C. Herman, *Destabilizing Milton: "Paradise Lost" and the Poetics of Incertitude* (New York: Palgrave Macmillan, 2008).

37. Stanley Fish, *How Milton Works* (Cambridge, MA: Belknap Press of Harvard University Press, 2003).

"What Hath Night to Do with Sleep?": Biopolitics in Milton's *Mask*

MELISSA E. SANCHEZ

This essay begins with the premise that Milton's *A Mask Presented at Ludlow Castle* makes legible the central, if usually tacit, role that sexual practice plays in both early modern and modern definitions of what it means to be human. In particular, *A Mask* – along with the religious and philosophical traditions that inform it and the critical discussions that have surrounded it – demonstrates the extent to which normative definitions of sex are based on a biopolitical temporality that shapes ontological distinctions between human and animal behavior. Comus, in many readings, is perverted and bestial because he flouts both normal daily rhythms (decent people work during the day and go to bed early) and normative developmental trajectories (one becomes a grown up only when one marries and has children). What these daily and developmental norms have in common is an orientation of one's sexual life toward future plans rather than present needs or pleasures. So one might say that what determines whether one is normal – or, to use the term most often employed by Milton and his critics, virtuous – is not only the gender of one's object choice but also the extent to which one practices the sexual restraint that sustains what Jack (Judith) Halberstam describes as the "narrative coherence of adolescence-early adulthood-marriage-reproduction-childrearing-retirement-death."[1] Such a chronology is a uniquely human aspiration. Indeed, Heidegger wondered whether the animal can be said to be "constituted by some kind of time" at all, given that it "merely has life," not the being-toward-death, the sense of anticipation and potentiality that defines *Dasein* and therefore humanity.[2] Read in the context of the philosophical and religious tradition that has shaped the outlook of both Milton and his modern critics, living in and for the present as Comus does, with its related choice of matter over spirit, this world over the next, becomes evidence not just of immaturity or perversion. In the estimation of the Lady and the Attendant Spirit, Comus's *carpe diem* sexuality signifies a failure to be fully human and therefore a relinquishment of the rights and privileges to which human being is entitled.[3]

The anxiety that sex transforms humans into beasts is, of course, central to the Circe myth on which *A Mask* is based. It is not only the Attendant Spirit, the Brothers, or the Lady who construe Comus's offers of present pleasure as a bad thing. With a few exceptions, Milton's readers have unanimously accepted the Spirit's and the Lady's evaluation of the pleasures, one might say the "lifestyle," that Comus promotes and therefore have inadvertently endorsed an ideology whose normative project queer theory uniquely allows us to appreciate.[4] I quote such readings at length in order to demonstrate the pervasiveness of an idealization of chastity among critics with otherwise very different arguments and methodologies. In describing Comus's association with Cotytto, William A. Oram suggests that, given classical and Renaissance associations of this goddess with transvestitism and licentiousness, the "befriending" that Comus asks of Cotytto "would seem to involve demonic possession which would result in a loss of rational control and a subsequent performance of goddess's bestial 'dues.'"[5] Stanley Fish describes sexual temperance as a "liberating action" in that it is "the sign of a refusal to be in bondage to natural processes and a declaration of dependence on a power that controls, and can at any time suspend, them."[6] Victoria Silver praises chastity as "a loving and reverent inflection towards the world and the body, the domains in which God, the soul, and their particular joy are made known."[7] Similarly, William Shullenberger applauds the Lady because she "effectively critiques and repudiates the pleasure package Comus has to offer, because she is able to envision and articulate a more compelling and comprehensive alternative," one of "mature womanhood" based on "the possibilities of a higher order of pleasure which chastity offers."[8] Feminist readings of *A Mask* have argued that chastity can liberate women not only from the excesses of libidinal drives, but also from the patriarchal constraints that chastity notionally sustains, and they have thereby implicitly sanctioned a normative suspicion that sex is innately dangerous and degrading.[9] Richard Halpern, for instance, notes that presence in *A Mask* of maenads, Amazons, and nymphs of Diana "mark the point at which virginity ceases to denote submission and begins to denote revolt."[10] John Rogers argues that the Lady offers an image of "self-sufficient femininity" that "functions to reconfigure the authoritarian dynamics of power in the world at large."[11] Kathryn Schwarz sees chastity as a compromised by nonetheless significant form of female agency that "might expose coercive normativity to its own double edge."[12]

    The point I want to make about such readings is not that they are inaccurate. To be sure, *A Mask* represents chastity much as these readers say it does. My observation, instead, is rather simple, even obvious. I want to point out that the idealization of chastity in *A Mask*, along with the philosophical and theological traditions from which it emerges, promotes heteronormativity insofar as it privileges certain sexual behaviors (those that are restrained, loving, monogamous, and procreative) over others (those that are uninhibited, anonymous, promiscuous, and nonprocreative). In reading *A Mask* through the framework of queer theory instead, we can appreciate how definitions of the human – along with the rights and privileges that we accord those who fit into that category and deny those who do not – are informed by what Elizabeth Freeman has called "chronopolitics," the shaping of biopolitical status through temporal mechanisms that determine which human experiences "officially count as a life or one of its parts."[13] In 1633, Milton acknowledged his own uneasy relationship to a normative timeline when he wrote a friend to contrast his desires for scholarly fame, which might require continued retirement from the world, with the "potent inclination in bred wch about this tyme of a mans life sollicits most, the desire of house & family of his owne to wch nothing is esteemed more helpefull then the early entring into credible employment, & nothing more hindering then this affected solitarinesse."[14] However much Milton may recognize "house & family" as what one *should* want at "this tyme of a mans life," his own inclination toward "solitarinesse" throws such normative logic into question.

Given that Milton wrote this letter so close to the composition of *A Mask*, we can understand this work as a meditation on the question of what constitutes normal and proper sexuality. Indeed, Shullenberger has rightly read *A Mask* as depicting the initiation of the Lady into sexual maturity.[15] Whereas Shullenberger, like most of Milton's critics, leaves unexamined the ideal of chastity to which the masque directs the Lady, I want to look more closely at the implications of this ideal, as well as the contradictions inherent within it.[16] For to queer Milton, as I understand it, is not just to look for his depictions of same-sex desire, though that is undoubtedly an important part of such a project. To queer Milton is also to examine his complex engagement with a heteronormative assumption that sex is most virtuous – indeed, most human – when it occurs between adults in a monogamous, loving, long-term, procreative relationship.

A queer reading of Milton, more specifically, helps us to challenge ideals of proper sexuality – and particularly what Michael Warner has called "the politics of sexual shame" – in the same way that feminist theory has helped us to question the gendered norms and hierarchies that Milton at times endorses.[17] As Warner has observed, "Perhaps because sex is an occasion for losing control, for merging one's consciousness with the lower orders of animal desire and sensation, for raw confrontations of power and demand, it fills people with aversion and shame." A queer ethics emerges not when we deny the shame of sex by insisting that it is entirely innocent and natural, "pleasurable and life-affirming."[18] Rather, "in those circles were queerness has been most cultivated, the ground rule is that one doesn't pretend to be *above* the indignity of sex. . . . A relation to others, in these contexts, begins in an acknowledgment of all that is most abject and least reputable in oneself."[19] We might compare Silver's assurance that "the Lady's predicament represents a way of dignifying human being without trying to escape it" with Warner's certainty that "If sex is a kind of indignity, then we're all in it together."[20] An awareness of the contrast between what we might call a reflexively normative ethics of sex and a consciously queer one allows us to question what Laurie Shannon calls "human exceptionalism," the notion that humanity is bounded off from all other creatures by virtue of our ability to rationalize and regulate our bodily functions.[21] For while *A Mask* certainly promotes a normative ethics of sex, it also shows that such an ethics cannot be sustained by the rationality that ostensibly separates human from beast. A normative sexual ethics, rather, rests on an appeal to a higher power that exceeds human reason and thereby exposes not only the limits of such reason but also the violence necessary to sustain a liberal humanist ideal of personhood and politics.

In *A Mask*, Comus makes visible an alternative way of being in the world, one that follows from reflection on what it means to embrace the dark and disturbing aspects of sexuality and one that the Spirit and the Lady cannot fully defeat or resist. I am not suggesting that Milton himself endorsed expressions of desire that we would now call "queer." Quite the opposite: I have no doubt that he would side with the Spirit and the Lady. But *A Mask* also acknowledges that chaste deferral may be no more rational than promiscuous indulgence – for the ultimate defense of the former depends not on reason but on a network of faith and violence that cannot be fully squared with the logic that ostensibly separates the human *cogito* from the *bête- machine*.[22]

The association of what Lee Edelman has called "reproductive futurism"[23] with humanity as such has a long history in Christian and Neoplatonic thought. A central figure in this history is St. Augustine, who locates the distinction between humans and beasts in the human ability to reflect on, theorize, and make value judgments about the sense perceptions that we share with animals. Whereas "the life of the lower animals consists entirely in the pursuit of physical pleasures and the avoidance of pains," to be human is to look to a future when the body's needs will be left behind: "we repair the daily wastage of our bodies by eating and drinking, until the time comes when you *will bring both food and our animal nature to an end* [1 Cor. 6.13] . . . But for the present I find pleasure in this need, though I fight against it, for fear of becoming its captive."[24] The truly happy life is always in the future, for "even the righteous man himself will not live the life he wishes unless he reaches that state where he is wholly exempt from death, deception, and distress, and has the assurance that he will for ever be exempt. This is what our nature craves, and it will never be fully and finally happy unless it attains what it craves."[25]

For the Neoplatonist philosophers whose influence permeates *A Mask*, this aspiration was a result of humanity's mixed nature.[26] In Pico's version of the creation myth, God made humanity "a creature of indeterminate nature" and instructed the first human that "thou mayest fashion thyself in whatever shape thou shalt prefer. Thou shalt have the power to degenerate into the lower forms of life, which are brutish. Thou shalt have the power, out of thy soul's judgment, to be reborn into the higher forms, which are divine." The Protestant Reformers were less optimistic about humanity's power to transcend what Ficino had called "the beast in us."[27] Accordingly, Luther and Calvin recommended marriage as the best way to redeem animal desires. As Luther allows, "in point of physical life there is no difference or very little difference between us and the animals . . . the only difference is that they have no reason."[28] For Luther, the thing that redeems the sexual impulse is the ability to contain it within procreative marriage:

> this word which God speaks, "Be fruitful and multiply," is not a command. It is more than a command, namely, a divine ordinance [*werck*] which it is not our prerogative to hinder or ignore. Rather, it is just as necessary as the fact that I am a man, and more necessary than sleeping and waking, eating and drinking, and emptying the bowels and bladder. It is a nature and disposition just as innate as the organs involved in it. Therefore, just as God does not command anyone to be a man or a woman but creates them the way they have to be, so he does not command them to multiply but creates them so that they have to multiply. And

> whenever men try to resist this, it remains irreversible nonetheless and goes its way through fornication, adultery, and secret sins, for this is a matter of nature and not of choice.[29]

The only proper way to give into the "nature and disposition" with which God has endowed humanity is to "multiply" oneself within the confines of marriage. But even married sex must not be too sexy. In the conjugal bed, Luther warns, "a man has to control himself and not make a filthy sow's sty of his marriage."[30] The sexual impulse is naturally to "multiply," not to find pleasure. To enjoy the work of procreation too much is to degenerate into a beast.

The Attendant Spirit's prologue and epilogue situate *A Mask* within a tradition that equates a futurist orientation with virtue and value, a presentist one with perversity and emptiness. He would therefore seem to epitomize the vulgar Platonism that Silver has critiqued as a mode of thought characterized by "the desire to escape mortality by transcending the embodied condition of our humanity and all those discomfiting circumstances that go with it."[31] Yet even as he longs for transcendence, the Spirit acknowledges its impossibility.[32] In the prologue, the Spirit appears incapable of disengaging himself from the earth; in the epilogue, he imagines a heaven defined by the distinctly worldly activities of marriage and procreation. The first sentence of *A Mask* oscillates between heaven and earth and aligns them with a series of oppositions – human and animal, future and present, eternity and immediacy – that will concern the work as a whole:

> Before the starry threshold of *Jove's* Court
> My mansion is, where those immortal shapes
> Of bright aerial Spirits live insper'd
> In Regions mild of calm and serene Air,
> Above the smoke and stir of this dim spot,
> Which men call Earth, and with low-thoughted care
> Confin'd and pester'd in this pinfold here,
> Strive to keep up a frail and feverish being,
> Unmindful of the crown that Virtue gives
> After this mortal change, to her true Servants
> Amongst the enthron'd gods on Sainted seats.
> Yet some there be that by due steps aspire
> To lay their just hands on that Golden Key
> That opes the Palace of Eternity:
> To such my errand is, and but for such,
> I would not soil these pure Ambrosial weeds
> With the rank vapors of this Sin-worn mold. (1-17)

The Spirit presents a grammatically complete sentence within the first line and a half, one that, despite its inverted syntax, contains a clear piece of information: "Before the starry threshold of *Jove's* Court / My mansion is." But then he continues the sentence for nine and a half more lines, only two and a half of which actually describe Jove's Court, their grammatical object. Notably, the Spirit is more interested in denigrating "this dim spot, / Which men call earth" than he is in celebrating "Regions mild of calm and serene Air": 7 out of 11 lines are about earth. However much the Spirit tries to escape the "pinfold" of earth, we might say that he himself remains "Confin'd and pester'd" there, revealing that it is not just the body but also the mind that is held captive by the "Sin-worn mold" that is at once the earth, the dirt that covers it, and the humanity that will gradually decay into the dust of which it was first formed. As in Augustine's analysis, the truly virtuous human strives not to sustain life, but to prepare for its end, when we will finally be "wholly exempt from death, deception, and distress." The temporal and spatial dimensions of the Spirit's speech thus come together: it is only "After this mortal change" that we can reach the serene place "Before Jove's Court" and "Above the smoke and stir of this dim spot." [33]

So what is it actually like at the "starry threshold of *Jove's* Court," the "Palace of Eternity"? To find out, we have to wait until the Spirit's epilogue. Here, we first learn that even the pleasures of the "Gardens fair / Of *Hesperus*" are inferior and temporary (981-982). The Spirit's description of "The *Graces*," "the rosy-bosomed *Hours*," and "*Iris* . . . with humid bow" frolicking in the flowers becomes more disturbing than delightful when these "Beds of hyacinth, and roses" are revealed as the place "Where young Adonis oft reposes, / Waxing well of his deep wound / In slumber soft" (986, 992, 998, 999). These "Gardens fair" are also the site of injury, death, and mourning insofar as they contain Venus and Adonis, whose adulterous relationship is ultimately located "on the ground" where Venus "Sadly sits" – mired, we can assume, in the "rank vapors of this Sin-worn mold" (1001, 1002). What initially seemed a description of fanciful delight and liberation from earthly care ends up only another version of the pinfold the Spirit disdains. The consolation is that there is a better world "far above in spangled sheen," one defined by marriage and procreation:

> Celestial *Cupid* her fam'd son advanc't,
> Holds his dear *Psyche* sweet entranc't
> After her wand'ring labors long,
> 'Till free consent the gods among
> Make her his eternal Bride,
> And from her fair unspotted side
> Two blissful twins are to be born,
> Youth and Joy; so *Jove* hath sworn.

Cupid and Psyche were allegories for Christ and the Soul in Neoplatonic philosophy, and their relationship was understood in conjugal terms.[34] This "eternal" union, the Spirit tells us, is possible only "After [Psyche's] wand'ring labors long," and the tense shifts of this epilogue paradoxically imagine such fruitful union as both accomplished and uncertain. Cupid "holds" Psyche in a present that has come "After" her labors, but the rest of the sentence is in the future conditional: this will not happen "*Till* free consent the gods among / *Make* her his eternal Bride," and the twins "are *to be* born" – or "so *Jove* hath sworn."

"What Hath Night to Do with Sleep?"

Like other of Milton's poems concerned with the gap between human time and divine eschatology, *A Mask* registers that gap in tense shifts: from a divine perspective of the *nunc stans*, this family has already been formed, even if from a human perspective its arrival must remain a matter of faith.

Such slippage from present to future makes legible the extent to which idealizations of chaste love pattern the heaven of the future on present, worldly institutions of marriage and procreation.[35] These institutions then proleptically acquire value and coercive force as a result of the future that they signify. Edelman has described the logic of reproductive futurism as one in which "all sensory experience, all pleasure of the flesh, must be borne away from this fantasy of futurity secured, eternity's plan fulfilled . . . . Paradoxically, the child of the two-parent family thus proves that its parents *don't* fuck and on its tiny shoulders it carries the burden of maintaining the fantasy of a time to come in which meaning, at last made present to itself, no longer depends on the fantasy of its *attainment* in time to come."[36] If we agree with John Leonard that "the Cupid and Psyche lines stand among the healthiest passages in Milton," we confuse vehicle and tenor and thereby identify the profoundly human constructs of marriage and reproduction with the divine order that ostensibly sanctions them.

But the corresponding escape from the irreducibly bestial and perverse aspects of all sex – whether within or outside marriage, monogamy, and romance – is ultimately unachievable, as the Spirit's depiction of Comus's temptations inadvertently admits. As we have seen, Augustine and Luther both recognized that however much bodily needs may be channeled into social institutions, these needs cannot be denied and therefore provide an insistent reminder of our animal nature. Indeed, as Laurie Shannon has argued, until Descartes formalized the distinction between the *cogito ergo sum*, the thinking human, on the one hand, and the *bête-machine*, the mechanical beast, on the other, there was no such thing as the blanket category of "the animal," a term which hardly appears in English before the end of the sixteenth century, as humanity's opposite. The operative model was instead Aristotle's *De Anima*, which endowed all things with a soul and postulated a taxonomy in which each higher form of life incorporated all kinds of souls below it. According to this model, human beings were higher than non-human animals but still on a continuum with them.[37] As the classical and early modern philosophical and theological traditions that I have sketched attest, distinctions between human and animal being had long been haunted by the possibility that the boundary could easily be crossed, that the human could degenerate into a beast (though beasts could never become human). For the Attendant Spirit, it is precisely this danger that Comus represents, for he

> Excels his Mother at her mighty Art,
> Off'ring to every weary Traveler
> His orient liquor in a Crystal Glass,
> To quench the drought of *Phoebus*, which as they taste,
> (For most do taste through fond intemperate thirst)
> Soon as the Potion works, their human count'nance,
> Th'express resemblance of the gods, is chang'd

"What Hath Night to Do with Sleep?"

> Into some brutish form of Wolf, or Bear,
> Or Ounce, or Tiger, Hog, or bearded Goat,
> All other parts remaining as they were.
> And they, so perfect is their misery,
> Not once perceive their foul disfigurement,
> But boast themselves more comely than before,
> And all their friends and native home forget,
> To roll with pleasure in a sensual sty. (63-77)

Although the Spirit initially describes the travelers' transformations as a result of Comus's "mighty Art," by the end of the passage it is clear that the travelers are more victims of their own somatic pressures than of Comus's diabolical power. Comus certainly offers the drink of "orient liquor in a Crystal Glass," but the travelers are "chang'd / Into some brutish form" as a result of their decision to "quench the drought of *Phoebus*." As Stephen Orgel has pointed out, it doesn't seem so bad to drink when one is thirsty: these people are "weary," after all, and parched by the heat of the sun.[38] Is thirst always "fond" and "intemperate," then, simply because it is a bodily need? In the Spirit's account, the answer would seem to be "yes." Even worse, the travelers are unable to tell what has really happened to them, misapprehending their "foul disfigurement" – their loss of human form – as a change that has made them "more comely than before." "Perfect misery" means a wretchedness or abjection so complete that it can no longer be perceived. What the travelers have lost is the Augustinian ability to find animal life unsatisfying and therefore to abandon the human circle of "friends and native home" in favor of a "sensual sty." As the Elder Brother will later concur, lust is its own punishment. By giving into the impulses of the body, one becomes increasingly subject to those needs. If one indulges lust "By unchaste looks, loose gestures, and foul talk, / But most by lewd and lavish act of sin," one loses the distinction between body and soul, as the soul "grows clotted by contagion, / Imbodies and imbrutes." This is the state of the undead, the spirit that remains on earth even after the demise of the body, "loath to leave the body that it lov'd, / And link't itself by carnal sensuality / To a degenerate and degraded state." Unchaste sex becomes a form of necrophilia – a pleasure in bodies emptied of the spirit or mind that defines "life."

Comus offers an alternative theory of sexuality. But rather than claim a utopian or transcendent approach to pleasure, Comus acknowledges abject and shameful aspects of sex. The "ugly-headed monsters" with which he is surrounded make visible, as the Lady claims, the bestial dimension of the life he lives – a dimension he makes no effort to repress or sublimate. The difference between Comus's approach, on the one hand, and the Lady's and the Spirit's, on the other, is not that the former is bestial and the latter human. The difference is that Comus admits the innate perversity of desire while the Lady and the Sprit believe that monogamous and procreative sex transcends the animal body with all its undignified drives and secretions. Comus's own first lines reject both the reproductive futurism that the Spirit endorses and the diurnal rhythms of "normal" adulthood. In his invocation of Cotytto, Comus emphasizes her ability to blur distinctions and collapse boundaries: she is "ne'er . . . call'd but when the Dragon womb / Of Stygian darkness spits her thickest gloom, / And makes one blot of all the air" (128, 131-133).[39] Imagining "thickest gloom" as the excretion of the "womb / Of Stygian darkness," Comus evokes the threat of the abject as Julia Kristeva has described it. For Kristeva, abjection is "what disturbs identity, system, order. What does not respect borders, positions, rules. The in- between, the ambiguous, the composite."[40] Abjection, in Kristeva's analysis, confronts us with the fragile states in which "man strays on the territory of the animal" and confronts "the hold of *maternal* entity before ex-isting outside of her."[41] Rejecting as it does moral and social limits, "Abjection then wavers between the *fading away* of all meaning and humanity . . . and the *ecstasy* of an ego that, having lost its Other and its objects, reaches, at the precise moment of this suicide, the height of harmony with the promised land."[42] This merging of human with earth – we might here recall the "Sin-worn mold" of the Spirit's prologue or the decaying corpses of the Elder Brother's speech – is at once terrifying and attractive. It signifies the same embrace of death that the Augustinian tradition of thought recommends, just without the transcendence.

Yet Comus's challenge to the boundaries on which subjectivity and society depend is as attractive as it is frightening.[43] For when he offers an alternative temporality, Comus also reveals how artificial and fragile are the normative ideologies that the Spirit espouses:

> What hath night to do with sleep?
> Night hath better sweets to prove,
> *Venus* now wakes, and wak'ns Love.
> Come let us our rites begin,
> 'Tis only daylight that makes Sin,
> Which these dun shades will ne're report. (93-114, 122-127)

In describing night as the time for pleasure rather than sleep, Comus rejects "normal" temporalities and boundaries as well as the values that adhere to them. The "Midnight shout and revelry / Tipsy dance and Jollity" that Comus describes is also a refusal of a normative ideal of maturity, the "Strict Age" that is marked by "Rigor," "Advice," "sour Severity" – and early bedtimes. We might think of Halberstam's description of queer time as "the dark nightclub, the perverse turn away from the narrative coherence of adolescence-early adulthood-marriage-reproduction-childbearing-retirement-death, the embrace of late childhood in place of early adulthood or immaturity in place of responsibility."[44] Read in the context of queer critiques of chronopolitics, Comus's rejection of Spirit's teleological schema also signifies a rejection of the heteronormative ideology such a schema upholds and naturalizes. For Comus, the way to approach both death and divinity is to ignore the "grave Saws" and instead "Imitate the Starry Choir," those heavenly bodies that are utterly indifferent to the human time that is based on their rotations. The "Months and Years" that measure out a life are merely a human interpretation of the heavens' meaning, not the secure ascent to "the starry threshold of *Jove's* Court" that the Spirit claims. In the "dun shades" of night, bodies and categories merge and the firm meanings that light might "report," or put into discourse, fade from view. These are not objective or constant realities but discursive formations of a value system that that has been constructed by the human imagination, not the divine fiat that heteronormative ideals and institutions claim merely to obey and enforce.

Comus similarly threatens the gendered and sexual orders on which the Spirit's idealization of the procreative family depend. Comus, notoriously, is "Much like his Father, but his Mother more" (57), and critics have seen this ambiguity as evidence of his degraded state. Fish derides him as a hermaphroditic momma's boy, while Louise Simons observes that Comus's wielding of Circe's cup and Bacchus's wand, iconic images of the female and male genitalia, announces that he has no clearly dominant sexual identity.[45] Ralph Singleton condemns Comus as "a gay sensualist and seducer."[46] Tracing representations of Comus's sexual ambiguity to classical, biblical, and Renaissance sources, on the one hand, and the scandalous sodomy trial of the Earl of Castlehaven, on the other, Ross Leasure describes Comus as a "predator of ambiguous sexuality on the prowl in hopes of seducing the Lady and victimizing her brothers."[47]

The critical condemnation of both gender ambiguity and same-sex desire in *A Mask* allows us to see how the seemingly neutral ideal of chastity can shore up connections between normative narratives of temporal development, human ontology, and sexual desire and practice. Particularly insofar as all of the other characters can be read as what Ann Baynes Coiro calls "refractions" of Comus, we can see his challenge to gender boundaries as a challenge to normative sexual values more largely.[48] Whereas Coiro deems *A Mask* "startlingly feminist," however, I would argue that the Spirit's and the Lady's denigration of sexuality must also be understood as denigrations of the feminine insofar as it has traditionally been aligned with the sensual, the particular, and the temporary as against the intellectual, the universal, and the eternal.[49] In Adorno and Horkheimer's analysis of the Circe myth, "the powerful seductress is at the same time weak, obsolete, and vulnerable" – and must remain so in order for rational man's domination of nature to be secured.[50] As Robyn Marasco has argued, Adorno and Horkheimer's analysis shows that the vilification of sex is the deprecation of "the only power formally granted to woman, rendering obsolete the power of female seduction and forcing upon her a new imperative: submit to civilization or remain outside of it." Moreover, because Odysseus's marriage to Penelope signals the completion of male domination over both women and the passions, "Circe's story stands as the point of transition, not from a feminine order to one of masculinist domination, but from the mythic power of sexuality to the triumph of sublimated rationality."[51] The "sublimated rationality" idealized by classical, Renaissance, and modern writers requires the demonization of the femininity, queerness, and animality that it seeks to transcend – or, failing transcendence, to destroy in the name of defending virtue. Comus challenges such a hierarchy not just in his attractiveness but, more importantly, in his insistent challenge to the logic of heteronormativity. For Milton's *Mask* ultimately shows that the chastity it advocates cannot be defended by recourse to rationality alone.

"What Hath Night to Do with Sleep?"

The debate between the Lady and Comus that is the centerpiece of *A Mask* disturbs the valuation of chastity that critics have let pass without comment and that continues to shape the biopolitical scripts through which Milton's work has been understood. The standard historical narrative is that companionate marriage constitutes a *via media* between two sexual options that mainstream Protestant Reformers discouraged: lifelong celibacy, on the one hand, and promiscuity, on the other. Indeed, as we have seen, Luther collapsed celibacy and promiscuity as two sides of the same coin, deeming the inevitably failed aspiration to virginity as the cause of "fornication, adultery, and secret sins." In the debate between Comus and the Lady, promiscuity is instead set off against both marriage and virginity. In response to the Lady's distinction between Comus's "lickerish baits fit to ensnare a brute" and "a draught for *Juno* when she banquets," a line that Leonard has convincingly argued celebrates marriage, Comus aligns marriage with virginity.[52] Both, he argues, attempt to deny the abjection of our creaturely desires and to project onto them a stable and coherent meaning. The result is that chastity, whether permanent or temporary, appears not as the recognition of our limitations but as a delusional attempt to escape uncertainty:

> List Lady, be not coy, and be not cozen'd
> With that same vaunted name Virginity;
> Beauty is nature's coin, must not be hoarded,
> But must be current, and the good thereof
> Consists in mutual and partak'n bliss,
> Unsavory in th'enjoyment of itself. (737-742)

The "mutual and partak'n bliss" that Comus recommends would appear to echo the Protestant ideal of companionate marriage, but Comus is careful to distinguish the lifestyle he has in mind from that initiated by "*Juno* when she banquets." His description of beauty – and the youth and pleasure it metonymically evokes – as currency embraces rather than denies the radical instability of bodily life. Like a coin, beauty has no intrinsic value or significance. The promiscuous circulation that Comus recommends threatens the clear structures of identity and stability for which both virginity and marriage strive. Whereas these forms of chastity remove us from circulation, and have clear definitions, promiscuity is defiantly erratic. In refusing to pretend that sex within some relations is inherently different from that within others, Comus admits and embraces the abjection of all human activity. Comus's earlier threat to make the Lady like "Root-bound" Daphne in this sense only literalizes the choice that in his view she is already making, that of stasis. As critics have observed, this predicament is an epitome of the earthly existence that the Spirit and the Elder Brother imagine as that of virtue: one in which we defer, or at least justify, carnal pleasure in the name of a future that is, really, only a matter of faith.

The conclusion of the debate between Comus and the Lady affirms that the reproductive futurism that *A Mask* espouses relies not on facts, logic, or evidence, but on an invocation of "some superior power" (800). Milton's Christian convictions are, of course, central to his writing, so it is hardly surprising that he ultimately substitutes divine rapture for human reason. What is surprising, however, is the absence of critical commentary on the significance of this substitution. For what the nonresolution of the debate demonstrates is that the ideology that *A Mask* celebrates is no more logical than the alternative view offered by Comus. The Lady does not emerge the clear winner of the argument. In fact, she cuts off the debate, charging in frustration that "thou art not fit to hear thyself convinc't" (792). She charges that Comus behaves as he does because he is what he is: precisely the sort of Cartesian *bête-machine* whose automatic, mindless response to the material world renders it inferior to those guided by reason and reflection. Remarkably, however, the Lady appeals not to the reason that is traditionally treated as the mark of humanity, but to something that sounds a lot like the irrational ecstasy that Comus endorses. Queer theory's critique of normative ideology allows us to see that the contest is not between human rationality and self-consciousness, on the one hand, and bestial sense and abjection, on the other. Rather, it is between two different perspectives on the proper response to the bodily needs and desires, not to mention the intellectual limitations, that thwart humanity's attempts fully to transcend animal existence. The Lady, notably, claims no agency or reason for herself – or anyone else. She warns, rather, that the "uncontrolled worth of this pure cause" will

> . . . kindle my rapt spirits
> To such a flame of sacred vehemence,
> That dumb things would be mov'd to sympathize,
> And the brute Earth would lend her nerves, and shake,
> Till all thy magic structures rear'd so high,
> Were shatter'd into heaps o'er thy false head. (792-799)

In the Lady's final words, "sacred vehemence" replaces secular reason. "[D]umb things" will be "mov'd to sympathize," and the passive construction of the sentence registers the passionate nature of this response. These "dumb things" may sympathize with the Lady, but they cannot articulate the reasons for their agreement. Similarly, the "brute Earth" will respond in the only way an irrational thing can: with brute force that destroys rather than persuades that which threatens it.

Comus may allow that the Lady's words are "set off by some superior power," but he refers not to the power of reason but the threat of physical violence, comparing his shaky and sweating reaction to that of "*Saturn's* crew" when "the wrath of *Jove* / Speaks thunder and the chains of *Erebus*" (800, 803, 801-802). He not persuaded by what he continues to characterize as "mere moral babble," and he resolves to "dissemble" his fear and "try her yet more strongly" (807, 805, 806). This is not, of course, to claim that Comus relies only on suasive reason. He tricks the Lady into following him, holds her against her will, and threatens her with physical and sexual violence, and as many feminists have pointed out, the sexual liberation he preaches may sustain masculine sexual privilege.[53] Rather, I want to point out that a feminist celebration of female chastity may unwittingly endorse the sexual moralism that has historically been used both to deny women sexual agency and to deny sexual minorities rights. Read in terms of ongoing debates between feminist and queer scholars, the exchange between Comus and the Lady reveals the limits of both a celebration of all sex as liberatory and a condemnation of all sex as disempowering.[54] Comus and the Lady have both resorted to physical force or its threat. Comus seems to recognize, as the Lady does not, that his victory will count only if he can persuade the Lady – for surely he could physically overcome her if that was what he really wanted. As Kathleen Wall has argued, "Comus does not want to rape [the Lady], he wants to *initiate* her."[55] The Lady's drinking, and the sexual initiation it signifies, will have a transformative effect only if she is the agent, however coerced her action may be. And while Comus certainly appeals to the same passions that the Lady evokes, promising "delight / Beyond the bliss of dreams," he also asserts the wisdom of accepting these passions. His final words, after all, are "Be wise, and taste." The two parts of this exhortation need not be seen as contradicting one another. Rather, Comus's conjunction of wisdom and taste challenges a Christian Neoplatonic framework by defining the acceptance of bodily appetites as a rational and judicious choice.

This helps explain why after the Lady is released, the Spirit urges that they "fly this cursed place, / Lest the Sorcerer *us* entice / With some other new device" (939-941, my emphasis). For, as we saw earlier, the Lady herself was attracted to "the sound / Of Riot and ill- manag'd Merriment" (171-172). Even as she insists that she "should be loath / To meet the rudeness and swill'd insolence / Of such late Wassailers" she heads right to the spot "Whence ev'n now the tumult of loud Mirth / Was rife and perfect in my list'ning ear" (177-179). And although she approaches these wassailers only in order to get help (and I think we should believe her on this), their presence does stir up "A thousand fantasies / . . . / of calling shapes and beck'ning shadows dire" (205, 207). As the Lady's subsequent lines make clear, these "calling shapes and beck'ning shadows dire" are also allegories of her own desires. The syntax of the clause, which defers the adjective "dire" until the end, suggests that the fear or foreboding aroused by these fantasies comes only as an afterthought to their alluring summons. As Shullenberger has beautifully put it, "the wood is the place where reason must come to terms with all that it is not, where the human discovers itself as an indeterminate question rather than a complacent assumption, where one meets oneself in forms one isn't prepared to recognize."[56] The Lady is, as critics have argued, rightfully furious at being held hostage. But her threats of violence also suggest the limits of the rationality for which she should stand, and therefore make her more like Comus than most critics have noticed.[57]

The Spirit's epilogue admits the inadequacy of the vision of *A Mask* on purely rational grounds. These closing lines assert instead the contradiction at the heart of the view that normal and perverse sex, along with the definitions of humanity and bestiality they sustain, are grounded on a contrast between rationality and irrationality, reflection and instinct. For this distinction ultimately cannot be upheld on the grounds of rationality and reflection alone. Rather, as the Lady, the Elder Brother, and the Spirit admit, and as Sabrina's necessary intervention attests, the equation of monogamous and procreative sex with virtue requires a supplementary appeal to a higher power. The final words of *A Mask*, like the Lady's final threat to Comus, accept that the virtue it has been celebrating is, ultimately, not available through human choice alone but requires divine intervention that may collapse rescue and retribution:

> Mortals that would follow me,
> Love virtue, she alone is free,
> She can teach ye how to climb
> Higher than the Sphery chime;
> Or if Virtue feeble were,
> Heav'n itself would stoop to her. (1018-1023)

Initially, the Spirit promises that virtue "alone is free," subject only to its own dictates, not external influence or force. But then he admits that virtue could turn out to be "feeble," too weak to stand on its own, so not quite "free." In this case, he assures us "Heav'n itself would stoop to her." Divided by that distinctly Miltonic "or," the Spirit's two definitions of virtue concede the limits of human rationality fully to defend the ideals it constructs without recourse to something beyond itself. And with that concession – one that Milton could not avoid, given his particular theological convictions – *A Mask* allows for a theory of sex that can rightly be called "queer" insofar as it undoes the clear distinctions between reason and passion, human and beast, and thereby opens a space within which we might question the biopolitical projects that such distinctions both naturalize and sustain.

Notes

I would like to thank the members of the audience at the University of Michigan conference on "Violence in the Early Modern Period" for their smart and helpful feedback on this essay. As always, Chris Diffee was an invaluable reader and listener throughout the writing process.

    1. "Theorizing Queer Temporalities: A Roundtable Discussion," *GLQ* 13 (2007): 177-195; 182. For an extensive critique of such a developmental ideal, see Lee Edelman, *No Future: Queer Theory and the Death Drive* (Durham: Duke University Press, 2004).
    2. *Being and Time*, trans. John Macquarie and Edward Robinson (New York: Harper and Row, 1962), 396.
    3. Jacques Derrida and Giorgio Agamben locate Heidegger's meditations on the question of what distinguishes the human from the animal in the specific ideological and political context in which he was writing (Derrida, *The Animal that Therefore I Am*, ed. Marie-Louise Mallet, trans. David Wills [New York: Fordham University Press, 2008], 127; Agamben, *The Open*, trans. Kevin Attell [Stanford: Stanford University Press, 2004], 75-77). Considering the problem across a longer history, Dorothy Yamamoto notes that some medieval theologians had argued that Jews could not really be human if they could not understand the dual nature of Jesus. She concludes that in this tradition, "Humanness may not be our birthright but may depend upon the exercise of a particular faculty," and asks "If such a faculty is *not* exercised, does it then cease to exist? And do we lose our purchase upon humanness as a result?" ("Aquinas and Animals: Patrolling the Boundary?", in *Animals on the Agenda*, 80-89).

"What Hath Night to Do with Sleep?"

4. One exception is Stephen Orgel, who locates the danger of Comus in the rejection of social, rather than metaphysical, virtues. See *Spectacular Performances: Essays on the Theatre, Imagery, Books and Selves in Early Modern England* (Manchester: Manchester University Press, 2011).

5. William Oram, "The Invocation of Sabrina," *SEL* 24 (1984): 121-139; 126.

6. Stanley Fish, "Problem Solving in *Comus*," in *How Milton Works* (Cambridge, MA: Belknap Press of Harvard University Press, 2001): 140-160; 156.

7. Silver, "Thoughts in Misbecoming Plight: Allegory in *Comus*," in *Critical Essays on John Milton*, ed. Christopher Kendrick (1995), 47-73; 68.

8. William Shullenberger, "Girl, Interrupted: Spenserian Bondage and Release in Milton's Ludlow *Mask*," *Milton Quarterly* 37 (2003): 184-204; 189, 185, 198. In addition, see Raymond G. Schoen, "The Hierarchy of the Senses in *A Mask*," *Milton Quarterly* 7 (1973): 32-37; Joan S. Bennett, "Virgin Nature in *Comus*," *Milton Studies* 23 (1987): 21-32; A. S. P. Woodhouse, "The Argument of Milton's *Comus*," in *A Masque at Ludlow: Essays on Milton's* Comus, ed. John Diekhoff (Cleveland: Press of Case Western Reserve University, 1968).

9. Feminist critics who have examined how the ideal of married chastity in *A Mask* constrains women's choices include Marcia Landy, "Kinship and the Role of Women in *Paradise Lost*," *Milton Studies* (1972): 3-18; and Julie H. Kim, "The Lady's Unladylike Struggle: Redefining Patriarchal Boundaries in Milton's *Comus*," *Milton Studies* 35 (1997): 1-20.

10. Richard Halpern, "Puritanism and Maenadism in 'A Mask,'" in *Rewriting the Renaissance: The Discourses of Sexual Difference in Early Modern Europe* (Chicago: University of Chicago Press, 1986), 88-105; 94.

11. John Rogers, *The Matter of Revolution: Science, Poetry, and Politics in the Age of Milton* (Ithaca: Cornell University Press, 1996), 118.

12. Kathryn Schwarz, "Chastity, Militant and Married: Cavendish's Romance, Milton's Masque," *PMLA* 118 (2003): 270-285; 281.

13. Elizabeth Freeman, "Time Binds, or, Erotohistoriography," *Social Text* 84-85 (2005): 57-68; 57.

14. *Complete Prose* 1.319. Leonard treats this as a confession that Milton was "open to the idea of marriage" and therefore as evidence that he embraced a heteronormative ideal of marriage as the best life (Leonard, "'Good Things': A Reply to William Kerrigan," *Milton Quarterly* 30 [1996]: 117-127; 126).

15. Shullenberger may be right that "the particular form of the Lady's socialization proves consonant with Milton's sense of the kind of adult character adequate to the challenges of his period," but we can nonetheless ask whether we want to celebrate this same idea of adulthood.

16. William Shullenberger, "Into the Woods: The Lady's Soliloquy in *Comus*," *Milton Quarterly* 35 no 1 (2001): 33-43; 34.

17. Michael Warner, *The Trouble with Normal: Sex, Politics, and the Ethics of Queer Life* (New York: Free Press, 1999), 74.

18. Warner, *The Trouble with Normal*, 2.

19. Warner, *The Trouble with Normal*, 35. Leo Bersani similarly proposes that accepting that sex involves impulses and practices that cannot be redeemed by narratives of love or pleasure encourages relinquishment of is ethical insofar as it compels us to relinquish the "sacrosanct value of selfhood, a value that accounts for human beings' extraordinary willingness to kill in order to protect the seriousness of their statements."

20. Warner, *The Trouble with Normal*, 35.

21. Laurie Shannon, "Invisible Parts: Animals and the Renaissance Anatomies of Human Exceptionalism," in *Animal Encounters*, ed. Tom Tyler and Manuela Rossini (Leiden: Brill, 2008), 137-157; 137.

22. While the Cartesian paradigm postdates the composition of *A Mask* by several years, it has been so influential on modern understandings of the human that I use it here as shorthand for the set of assumptions that this essay interrogates. For discussions of Descartes influence, see Laurie Shannon, "The Eight Animals in Shakespeare, or, Before the Human," *PMLA* 124 (2009): 472-479; Derrida, *The Animal that Therefore I Am*; and Bruce Boehrer, *Animal Characters: Nonhuman Beings in Early Modern Literature* (Philadelphia: University of Pennsylvania Press, 2010), 8-10, 16-17.

23. Edelman, *No Future*, 2.

"What Hath Night to Do with Sleep?"

24. Augustine, *On Free Choice of the Will*, trans. Thomas Williams (Hackett, 1993), 14, and *Confessions*, trans. R. S. Pine-Coffin (Harmondsworth: Penguin, 1961),10.31. See also Gillian Clark, "The Fathers and the Animals: The Rule of Reason?", in *Animals on the Agenda*, ed. Andrew Linzey and Dorothy Yamamoto (London: Illini, 1998), 69, 76.

25. Augustine, *Concerning the City of God Against the Pagans*, trans. Henry Bettenson (Harmondsworth: Penguin, 1972),14.25.

26. Giovanni Pico della Mirandola, *Oration on the Dignity of Man*, trans. Elizabeth Livermore Forbes, in *The Renaissance Philosophy of Man*, ed. Ernst Cassirer, Paul Oskar Kristeller, and John Herman Randall, Jr (Chicago: University of Chicago Press, 1948), 224-225.

27. Discussion of I Cor. 15 in *Luther's Works* (St. Louis and Philadelphia, 1958-86), 28.189.

28. Discussion of I Cor. 15 in *Luther's Works* (St. Louis and Philadelphia, 1958-86), 28.189.

29. *The Estate of Marriage*. [1522] Trans. Walther I Brandt.

30. *A Sermon on Estate of Marriage*, 415. Similarly, Calvin warned that "This excess Ambrose censured gravely, but not undeservedly, when he described the man who shows no modesty or comeliness in conjugal intercourse, as committing adultery with his wife" (*Institutes of the Christian Religion*, trans. Henry Beveridge [Peabody, MA: Hendrickson, 2008], 8.44). For a fuller discussion of the contradictions inherent in Reformation views of marriage, see Melissa E. Sanchez, "'Modesty or Comeliness': The Predicament of Reform Theology in Spenser's *Amoretti and Epithalamion*," *Renascence* 65 (2012): 5-24.

31. Silver, "Thoughts in Misbecoming Plight," 71. For readings that would have Milton adhering to this version of Platonism, see Sears Jayne, "The Subject of Milton's Ludlow Mask, in *Milton: Modern Essays in Criticism*, ed. Arthur Barker (Oxford: Oxford University Press, 1965); and Fish, "Problem Solving in Comus."

32. For another reading of this oddity, see Fish, "Problem Solving in *Comus*."

33. The Spirit's cosmography echoes that of Pico: "The region above the heavens He had adorned with Intelligences, the heavenly spheres He had quickened with eternal souls, and the excrementary and filthy parts of the lower world He had filled with a multitude of animals of every kind" (224).

34. See Edgar Wind, *Pagan Mysteries in the Renaissance* (London: Faber and Faber, 1968), 160-176.

35. As Halpern notes, "In *A Mask*, heavenly bliss seems to be only a trope for wedded bliss" ("Puritanism and Maenadism," 97).

36. Edelman, *No Future*, 40-41.

37. Shannon, "The Eight Animals in Shakespeare." See also Derrida, who examines the "mutation" between Montaigne, who attributed to animals a capacity for reason, and Descartes (*The Animal that Therefore I Am*, 6-7), and Boehrer's argument that the Cartesian *cogito* sought to resolve an early modern crisis of distinction (*Animal Characters: Nonhuman Beings in Early Modern Literature* [Philadelphia: University of Pennsylvania Press, 2010], 1-27). Agamben sees the taxonomic shift happening later, with the nineteenth-century development of the human sciences (*The Open*, 23-27). The Cartesian model has recently been cast into doubt by the field of animal studies. Along with Shannon and Derrida, see Donna Haraway, *Cyborgs, Simians, and Women: The Reinvention of Nature* (New York: Routledge, 1990), 1-42 and *When Species Meet* (Minneapolis: University of Minnesota Press, 2009); Cary Wolfe, *Zoontologies: The Question of the Animal* (Minneapolis: University of Minnesota Press, 2003); and Matthew Calarco, *Zoographies: The Question of the Animal from Heidegger to Derrida* (New York: Columbia University Press, 2008).

38. Orgel, *Spectacular Performances*, 117. Will Stockton has rightly argued that in *A Mask* sex is not limited to genital penetration but includes a range of corporeal drives and pleasures, so that *all* bodily appetites become saturated with libidinal and moral significance ("The Seduction of Milton's Lady," in *Sex Before Sex: Figuring the Act in Early Modern Literature*, ed. Will Stockton and James Bromley [Minneapolis: University of Minnesota Press, 2012], 233-61).

39. See, for instance, Oram, and Maryann Cale McGuire, *Milton's Puritan Masque* (Athens: University of Georgia Press, 1983), 150.

40. Julia Kristeva, *Powers of Horror: An Essay on Abjection*, trans. Leon S. Roudiez (New York: Columbia University Press, 1982), 4.

41. Kristeva, *Powers of Horror*, 12-13.

42. Kristeva, *Powers of Horror*, 18.

43. Other critics who have noted Comus's attractiveness include Rosemary Tuve, "Image, Form, and Theme" in *A Mask*," in Diekhoff, 138; and Orgel, *Spectacular Performances*, 121.

44. Halberstam, "Theorizing Queer Temporalities," 182.

45. Fish, "Unblemished Form," in *How Milton Works*, 172-175; Louise Simons, "'And Heaven Gates Ore My Head': Death as Threshold in Milton's Masque," *Milton Studies* 23 (1987): 53-96; 61-62.

46. Ralph Singleton, "Milton's *Comus* and the *Comus* of Erycius Puteanus," *PMLA* 58 (1943): 949-957: 950.

47. Ross Leasure, "Milton's Queer Choice: Comus at Castlehaven," *Milton Quarterly* 36 no. 2 (2002): 63-86.

48. Ann Baynes Coiro, "'A Thousand Fantasies:' The Lady and the *Maske*," in *The Oxford Handbook of Milton*, ed. Nicholas MacDowell and Nigel Smith (Oxford: Oxford University Press, 2010), 89-111.

49. Coiro, "'A Thousand Fantasies,'" 89.

50. Max Horkheimer and Theodor Adorno, *Dialectic of Enlightenment*, ed. Gunzelin Schmid Noerr, trans. Edmund Jephcott (Stanford: Stanford University Press, 2002), 56.

51. Robyn Marasco, "'Already the Effect of the Whip?': Critical Theory and the Feminine Ideal," *differences* 17 no 1 (2006): 88-115; 96, 97. For an example of the equation of virtue with sexual continence and masculinity, see Fish's approving observation that "the Lady has internalized the father's authority and identifies with him so strongly that her feminine nature has been wholly subordinated" ("Unblemished Form," 172).

52. Leonard, "'Good Things,'" 122-124.

53. As Leah Marcus and John Leonard have rightly pointed out, this is hardly as situation in which both parties in the debate have equal freedom and power. See Leonard, "Saying 'No' to Freud: Milton's *A Mask* and Sexual Assault," *Milton Quarterly* 25 no 4 (1991): 129-140; 133; Leah Marcus, "The Milieu of Milton's *Comus*: Judicial Reform at Ludlow and the Problem of Sexual Assault," *Criticism* 25 (1983): 293-327; 317. See also Silver, who argues that the Lady's anger is intelligible in light of the real bodily injury she has received ("Thoughts in Misbecoming Plight," 70).

54. Feminists, that is, have long accused queer scholars with misogyny and the assumption of masculine privilege, while queer scholars have charged feminists with homophobia and reactionary sexual moralism. For examples, see, respectively, Dympna Callaghan, "The Terms of Gender: 'Gay' and 'Feminist' *Edward II*," in Feminist Readings *of Early Modern Culture: Emerging Subjects*, ed. Valerie Traub, M. Lindsay Kaplan, and Dympna Callaghan (Cambridge: Cambridge University Press, 1996), 275-301; and Jonathan Goldberg, "Introduction," in *Queering the Renaissance*, ed. Jonathan Goldberg (Durham, NC: Duke, 1994), 1-14.

55. Kathleen Wall, *The Callisto Myth from Ovid to Atwood: Initiation and Rape in Literature* (McGill-Queen's Press, 1988), 57. See also Tuve, "Image, Form, and Theme," 148.

56. Shullenberger, "Into the Woods," 35.

57. As even Fish admits, "the energy [Milton] must deploy in order to shore up and support the structure whispers to us of its precariousness and of the extent to which the purity he celebrates is finally inseparable from the materiality he pushes away" ("Unblemished Form," 184).

Dagon as Queer Assemblage: Effeminacy and Terror in *Samson Agonistes*

DREW DANIEL

Introduction: The Foul Yoke of Effeminacy

Though it is now many years since the original controversy erupted with John Carey's assertion in a review of Stanley Fish's *How Milton Works* that "September 11 has changed *Samson Agonistes*," the repercussions of this fractious public debate continue to inflect how the work is read at the present time.[1] In the wake of this polarizing conflict, interpretation of the poem as a complex whole has been upstaged by an urgent pressure to critically avow or disavow Samson's final action as either divinely inspired or pathological, with the tantalizingly over-determined massacre of the assembled Philistines in the temple of Dagon functioning for both sides as evidence for – or against – an authorial endorsement of the spectre of "terrorism" allegedly mobilized within Milton's closet drama. What are we to make of the "rousing motions" that lie at the core of this poem's central moment of decision? How might the possibilities of a "queer Milton" or, for that matter, a "queer Samson," reorient this seemingly intractable crux? It is my gambit that a consideration of the constitutive links between effeminacy and terror – links I shall trace both across the Miltonic corpus and within its titular character – might allow us to rethink recent critical traffic between *Samson Agonistes* and the security state by exposing a queer logic of near-resemblance through which Milton's text both solicits and frustrates typological expectation.

Samson Agonistes (1671) establishes a rhythmic emotional pattern in which hopeful visitors try to draw Samson out of his thing-like withdrawal, and are rewarded with either brutally reflexive rejection or violent threats. To (briefly) rehearse the dramatic sequence of events: His father Manoa proposes that a ransom be paid in order to liberate Samson from enslavement, tempting him with the possibility of a return home. His estranged wife Dalila seeks reconciliation, and tries to tempt him with the promise of "conjugal affection." The brute Harapha tries to tempt Samson into single combat to determine the relative supremacy of the god of Israel against a pagan challenger. Finally, his captors try to tempt Samson to display his strength and submission for the Philistine elite. This dialogic sequence of temptations refused cumulatively builds an affective tension between violence and compliance that leads to the work's notorious catastrophe. After a mysterious transformation in which "I begin to feel / Some rousing motions in me which dispose / To something extraordinary my thoughts," Samson permits himself to attend the enemy's "holy day" (1381-83).² His ironic performance of pseudo- submission culminates in an offstage act of horrific violence: Samson pulls down the pillars that support the theater-like structure in which the Philistine nobility are celebrating their triumph, in the process destroying the feast of Dagon and himself.

If these potentially compromising temptations loosely parallel the series of temptations rejected by Christ in the poetic drama's textual partner, *Paradise Regained*, the intended consequence of that typological pressure remains subject to a curiously restricted pair of options: typology or anti-typology, a binary that drives even Julia Lupton's show-stopping critical formulation that "Milton's Samson is finally not typological (a figure of Christ), or even typological in a terminally suspended way ("exil'd from light"), but *anti-typological*, arresting the recuperative moment of typology in the sheer violence of his act."³ Faced with a choice between a Samson that resembles Christ and a Samson that deliberately fails to sustain such a resemblance, I want to risk a question that is deliberately impertinent to the prevailing debate: how might the queer textual experience of Samson's effeminacy complicate the problem of typological resemblance itself? Going further, how might the pursuit of this question open out both the conjunctive disjunction of Milton studies with queer studies, and the sticky relevance of *Samson Agonistes* to the security state it supposedly prefigures?

Samson's stony, stoic refusals, and the upsurge of superhuman athleticism that overwhelms them, have together consolidated his identity as the definitive avatar of masculine fortitude, the *idée reçu* of the strong, silent type. Milton has other ideas. Far from impregnable and self-evident, in *Samson Agonistes* Samson's manhood is marked first and foremost by a persistent anxiety about its capacity to betray itself and transform into a disastrously compromising effeminacy. Tracking this as a historical structure with critical effects upon the present, in this essay as a whole I shall move between "manhood" and "masculinity" as the gendered term against which Samson's "effeminacy" shows up as its threatening structural inversion. For my purposes, "manhood" should be understood not only in relation to boundaries of gender but also to boundaries of ethos, polis and species; in early modernity, the opposite of manhood is not (only) "womanhood" or "femininity" but also in-civility, brutality, animality, in- humanity.⁴ The conceptual space of the "un-manly" thus constitutes a negative reserve in which class, ethnicity, species, and gender differences mutually figure each other, and reservoirs of meaning from any of these separate registers can flow into the space opened up within manhood by effeminacy.

Anxiety about the inward contamination of male gender by effeminate possibility constitutes a thread of queer fear that runs throughout Milton's poetry and his prose, taking different local forms each time, but sharing a family resemblance with its locus classicus, the angelic reproach in *Paradise Lost* directed at "Man's effeminate slackness" (11.632). Samson's self-hatred focuses its energy through an insistent proclamation of the "effeminacy" he supposedly demonstrated in succumbing to Dalila's demands that he reveal the secret of his strength:

> At times when men seek most repose and rest,
> I yielded, and unlocked her all my heart,
> Who with a grain of manhood well resolved
> Might easily have shook off all her snares:
> But foul effeminacy held me yoked
> Her bond-slave. O indignity, O blot
> To honor and religion! Servile mind
> Rewarded well with servile punishment! (406-413)

Samson's scenario of "yielding" and "unlocking" in the night summons up the remorseful laments of despoiled maidens bewailing the loss of their virginity – but ironically what has been lost here (momentarily displaced? forever dissolved?) is not maidenhood, but "manhood." The reference to other men as a class marks Samson as somehow cut off from homosocial solidarity, defenseless against his own servile gullibility. "Holding" him against his will, effeminacy is made here into an agent whose foul embrace cannot be withstood.[5]

Here we must attend to a discrepancy in the signification of "effeminacy" itself within the period. The term could designate a male with "womanly" characteristics, its first meaning, but it could also signify a male with an inordinate weakness *for* women; as the OED notes in reference to usage in Caxton (1460) and Puttenham (1589), "the notion 'self-indulgent, voluptuous' seems sometimes to have received a special colouring from a pseudo-etymological rendering of the word as '*devoted to women*'. Unequivocal instances are rare."[6] If we keep this second definition in mind, then Samson's self-accusation may simply be directed at his gullibility, and his indulgence of his wife. Certainly the Biblical source in the book of Judges sounds this note, with its joke-like repetition of Dalila's demand for Samson's secret eventually producing the desired revelation in a disastrous display of credulity. Secondarily speaking, "effeminate" could simply be a synonym for "uxorious."

Yet the capacity of the meaning of effeminacy in the period to slide between its two distinct definitions also usefully marks an ambient difference between early modern understandings of gender and normative (if equally debatable) "modern" schemas of sexual orientation. In our own cultural moment, in which we are subject to the reified sexological categories of heterosexuality and homosexuality and are schooled by popular psychology to probe for the occulted undersides of how those locations manifest themselves in everyday life, an "effeminate" male potentially falls under suspicion of so-called "latent" or unacknowledged homosexuality in a manner compatible with the first meaning but necessarily incongruous with the second. By contrast, for early modern subjects the polarities of "masculine" and "feminine" stand in a more volatile relationship as, on the one hand, social positions structured by rigid and divinely ordered prescriptions about rule and obedience, and, on the other, developmental outcomes placed by classical physiology into an entangling proximity.

Effeminacy's second definition within early modernity draws its strength from a historically distinct morphological imaginary sourced, ultimately, in a classical inheritance. Samson's sense of effeminacy as an invasion from within recalls John J. Winkler's formulation of sex and gender in classical Mediterranean culture as one in which "'woman is not only the opposite of man; she is also a potentially threatening 'internal émigré' of masculine identity."[7] Such a possibility might be said to constitute the bad dream of the so-called "One Sex model" so widespread within New Historicist readings of Galenic physiology in the wake of Thomas Laqueur's seminal *Making Sex*. If women are only born women because of their stalled developmental progress within the womb en route to becoming men, might it not also be possible that "from within" a man might somehow lapse and slide backwards towards another gendered location? This is the inverse scenario to the hermaphroditic possibility that animates that touchstone of New Historicist thought on the swerves and curves of gender normativity, Steven Greenblatt's "Fiction and Friction" in *Shakespearean Negotiations*, in which sufficient heat permits the extroversion of "Marie" le Marcis's female genitals into their final, normative male form as the male genitals of Marin le Marcis.[8] If the pseudo-revolt of transvestite theater described therein through Greenblatt's reading of Viola occurred under the protective shade of a normative masculine superiority, then, framed against this New Historicist critical rubric, the effeminate male is the early modern gender system's worst possible outcome. This is so not because he is a figure neither successfully masculine nor authentically feminine (granting that such secondary authenticity is in a peculiar sense impossible given the inherent insufficiency of the feminine position), but because, as a backslider, he is the only agent capable of betraying the forward course of masculine supremacy itself. Loitering with intent in a contaminating interstitial space between genders, the early modern effeminate man is a gender recusant.

Acutely afraid of his own effeminacy but also eager to self-consciously punish himself for it, Samson seems at pains to accuse himself of specifically the second kind of effeminacy – but he risks protesting too much in the process, and his accounts of that condition slide uncomfortably "forwards" (proleptically, historically) towards the first definition, with its connotations of a contaminating inward marker of feminine qualities and, specifically, with a feminine "weakness" in the face of sexual advances. In Samson's imagination, this state capaciously opens itself to suggestions of anal rape and military dramas of subjection, captivity, and male homoeroticism. The self-accusation of "effeminacy" recurs in Samson's thoughts on the uselessness of a merely occasional temperance in a manner which telegraphs his terror at occupying a permissive, receptive, passive position: "What boots it at one gate to make defense, / And at another to let in the foe / Effeminately vanquished?" (560-562). The "other gate" in this image is an unexpected entryway into one's self. In this military scenario (the image is one of attackers penetrating a town's line of defense) "to be conquered" and "to be effeminate" somehow lead to and verify each other. Effeminacy makes one a ripe and justified target for conquest, and having been conquered confirms and ratifies that effeminacy, securing a lasting shame for the vanquished by retroactively projecting a prior condition felt to somehow merit domination as its confirming response.

What relationships might there be between this foundational terror about the masculine self's inbuilt feminine possibility and other forms of terror, in particular terror at – not to mention acts of terror against – the unseen multitude of racial, religious, and sexual others which crowd in at an uncertain distance around the blind Samson? What are the links between the public display of Samson as the shaved and humiliated prisoner of war and his own anxiety about the loss of manhood? To what extent does Dagon's formal hybridity incite or call forth an act of terror from Samson, and in what way might this response index a certain constitutive linkage or provoking resemblance between effeminate manhood and pagan assemblage?

In pursuit of some provisional answers to these questions, I intend to borrow some critical tools from recent queer studies, not without some anxiety of my own. I adapt the phrase "queer assemblage" and its partners "terrorist assemblage" and "terrorist look-alike" from Jasbir Puar's work on the mutually reinforcing homophobic and xenophobic logics (or, if you prefer, anxieties) in play within certain persistent acts of violence taking place under the shadow of the overarching and, yes, ongoing "war on Terror."[9] In the related figures of the terrorist look-alike and the suicide bomber Puar identifies two manifestations of a politically and racially volatile form of queerness, one that alternately embodies violence and triggers pre-emptive or compensatory acts of violence in response to the ambient anxieties of the new security state. The exploding bodies of a suicide bomber-and-their-bystanders constitute a "terrorist assemblage" that violently re-organizes human and machine, flesh and explosive, criminal agent and victim, body and urban space, leveling and mixing and reforming both individual bodies and social bodies through radical acts of transformation. In Puar's analysis, "Terrorist look-alikes" and "queer assemblages" denote less an identifiable sexual / racial / religious / cultural category than a vertiginous failure of social location and the opening up of a threateningly non-specific possibility that constitutes what is "queer" now about those bodies that do not allow an implied patriotic "us" to feel safe.

In the first case, the figure of the "terrorist look alike" (say, a turbaned man in an airport) induces a panicked proceduralism about the universality of security screening in response to a de facto profiling which anxiously overlays virtual terrorism onto racialized bodies and faces. By contrast, "queer assemblage" is broader in scope and application, but in a particularly forceful reading Puar's text considers the joining of bodies and turbans in Sikh masculinity as a combinatorial assemblage in a Deleuzian sense: the interface fashioned between fabric and flesh constitutes an essenceless concatenation of materials with expressive consistency across a range of examples distributed across geographic space and political history, making the resulting point of contact into a constant site of becoming and intensification.[10] This particular assemblage is queer twice over, insofar as its presentation troubles gendered norms and in the process snarls the matrices of gender identity and citizenship/national identity. As conceptual assemblages themselves, Puar's terms can seem highly unstable: are they descriptions of bodies or descriptions of the ideologically framed ways in which bodies show up for (paranoid, hostile) spectators? Do they describe a political situation or a prevalent phobic response to a political situation?

Describing racist attacks on Sikh men in the wake of 9/11, Puar's analysis flags the symbolic importance of forcibly removing hair in a manner that inadvertently recalls the symbolic subjection of the captured, shaved and blinded Samson:

> It is not for nothing that in one hate crime incident after another, turbans are clawed at viciously, and hair is pulled, occasionally even cut off. The intimacy of such violence cannot be overstated. The attack functions as a double emasculation: the disrobing is an insult to the (usually) male representative (Sikh or Muslim) of the community, while the removal of the hair entails submission by and to normative patriotic masculinities.[11]

While in this particular context the subject of this violence is the (mis)recognized Sikh male wrongly accused and attacked for summoning up the anxiety of a nonspecific but endlessly imminent terrorist threat in their onlookers (finally, a wished for end to the threat level orange cloud of unknowing implication in which we live), in her work as a whole the term "queer assemblages" seems to designate a field of affect magnetized by the tension between two related but opposed positions and the bodies that occupy them: the "terrorist look-alike" body of the turbaned Sikh male, and the "terrorist assemblage" of the suicide bomber, a body that is comprised of organic and inorganic materials, a hybrid creation of machine/flesh set to violently reconfigure urban space. The difficulty of the term is that each body in and of itself constitutes a "queer assemblage," but each functions through the total field of quasi-legibility which their capacity to stand for each other generates (the fear generated by the civic circulation of the supposed "terrorist look-alike" might be the primary site through which the imagined body of the "suicide bomber" operates more effectively to claim social/psychic territory than in any particular site of explosion), and so in a sense *this differential field too constitutes a "queer assemblage."* Each term triggers their own queer effects, and each occupies a contested zone of signification within the ongoing war on terror – for the queer critic no less than for the subject of "normative patriotic masculinity."

As Jasbir Puar extends the term, queerness has more to do with a certain affective indeterminacy than it does to any available taxonomy of legible sexual practices. In resonant sympathy with both the work of Lee Edelman, Jack Halberstam, Madhavi Menon and others, for Puar queerness is not an identity one comfortably inhabits but a charge set off by what does not scan, what shows up as somehow other; her work accordingly seeks out queerness in "the unexpected, the unplanned irruptions, the lines of flight, the denaturalizing of expectation."[12] At this political moment, what could be less reassuring than the "Monster-Terrorist-Fag," Puar and Amit Rai's term of art for the absolutely inassimilable figure of the "terrorist look-alike" caught in the glance of the security guard, the potentially queer body of the turbaned Sikh male whose turban (like and unlike a headscarf) is said to induce a layered pair of interpretive anxieties (potentially female? potentially terrorist?) for its onlookers. The queer assemblage of the "monster-terrorist-fag" is felt to anchor by contrast the normative patriotic masculinity of both straight society and, in a decisive turn for Puar's analysis, a privileged (white) body of gay and lesbian "proud Americans" who are by contrast eager to vouch for their fealty to neoliberal tolerance in opposition to a Muslim outside now reified as inherently un-and-anti-queer. This implicitly Islamophobic polarity of affiliation conscripts the "properly queer" liberal and racialized subjects – piously invoked in every LGBTQ rollcall – into service as supposed victims under threat from Arab, Sikh, Muslim and South Asian communities, in the process erasing the existence of queers from those groups and tacitly pinkwashing Western democracies.[13] This framing constitutes a second differential field: the "queer assemblage" of anxiety and reaction that separates the "homonationalist" community from its rejected "terrorist look-alikes."

"Queer assemblages" do not show up in a triumphalist claiming of individual voices or communities but in moments of rupture in the socially negotiated; the assemblage is not an assembly, the communal or ghetto-ized safe space for consumption staked as a freehold within heteronormativity. "Queer assemblage" designates a corporeal, sexual, technological, cultural and historical manifold and tries to keep in play the queer body's provisional status as an arrangement open to interpretation and subject to change: bodies extended in time (think of the passages a transgendered body has undergone as an arc of becoming), bodies marked by violence, bodies marked by choice. It refers to, but does not capture and contain, an account of the queer body as a hybrid body, a part-object, something supplemented, perhaps enhanced, modified, or altered, something un-natural, a somatic border area with all gates open.

Accordingly, in invoking "Dagon as queer assemblage," I am relying upon this elasticity in order to bring out more fully the somatic queerness of Dagon as a node in the terrified / fascinated imagination of John Milton, and of Samson within Milton's work. That is, Dagon's mixture into "one" body of elements both male and female, human and animal, monstrous sovereign deity and humiliated victim of torture, represents the entirely corporeal and somatic quintessence of sin-saturated embodiment, but it does so as an assemblage that is "in some sense machined-together": this "sea-idol" is both a poetic construction and yet also the flesh-iest form that flesh can take, occupying the farthest and lowest point from, say, the angelic trans-sexuality imagined in *Paradise Lost*.

In relocating Puar's terms and impressing them into service in a reading of seventeenth century religious drama, I am producing a necessarily wrenching and "forced" cutting and re- assemblage of elements from Milton scholarship and queer studies into an encounter that will no doubt seem rather suspect from certain locations on both sides of this divide. But I hope to justify such hostage-taking. When read in terms of the overdetermined significations within its scriptural origin(s), and in the cluster of anxieties about sexuality which show up within Milton's creative re-use of this pagan god, Dagon's bodily form shows up as a "queer assemblage" sourced trans-historically from an anachronistic series of layered meanings, species and genders. But the same can be said for Dagon's nemesis. A shaved and humiliated political prisoner put on display by a foreign power in an attempt to further disenfranchise a subject people, an anxiously hyper-masculine hero prone to passionate displays of self-hatred for the taint of effeminacy, Samson shows up as both a "queer assemblage" to himself and a "terrorist look-alike" for contemporary criticism, insinuating himself into public space and then destroying it.[14] Alternately absolutely powerless and absolutely powerful, in its capacious overtaking of boundary conditions Samson's body reduplicates the formal hybridity of Dagon: a blind-yet-illuminated mind buried within a body that acquires and loses traits of both genders, a body that partakes of creaturely conditions at the border between the animal and the human, a body frozen in postures of living death and roused by inward motions of divine fury.

Milton Studies vs. Queer Studies: a "Clash of Civilizations"?

Faced with the claim that Milton's literary representations of Dagon and Samson "show up as" queer assemblages, one may well be tempted to ask "for whom?" Though perhaps this special issue will prove the contrary, at this point Milton studies and queer studies appear to have little to say to each other. That this is so emerges from a perhaps not accidental historical divide, and is compounded by the habits and tendencies peculiar to both camps. To state the obvious: the first waves of "queer theory" were consolidated around the reading of British and American nineteenth century literature and culture in dialogue with and informed by, however much they critiqued or expanded, Foucault's *History of Sexuality, Volume I*, and were marked by an oft-simplified and widely disseminated assertion supposedly found therein concerning the nineteenth century sexological origins of homosexual identity qua medically legible category of personhood.[15] The ensuing early modern critical responses and correctives, from Bruce R. Smith, Jonathan Goldberg, Mario DiGangi, Richard Rambuss, Madhavi Menon and others tended to concentrate upon the drama of Shakespeare and Marlowe, or the lyric poetry of Barnfield and Spenser, usefully bringing the nineteenth century homosexual into an uncannily disjunctive historical/critical relationship with the anticipatory but distinct figure of the early modern sodomite. Yet in all the fertile and ongoing work to read and theorize about same-sex desire in early modern culture, Milton seems, all too frequently, conspicuously absent from the discussion. Given the otherwise voluminous amount of work on sex and gender in Milton's writing, such a lacuna still needs explaining.[16] I would venture to suggest that this scholarly no-go area has everything to do with the tenor of Milton scholarship, in which a constitutive anxiety about "ruining the sacred truths" and a vexed awareness of the watchful paternal gaze of an authorial super-ego seems, still, to inhibit the scene of critical investigation when the subject is sexuality.

There are exceptions to this rule, notably Gregory Bredbeck's *Sodomy and Interpretation: From Marlowe to Milton* (1991) as well as articles by Jonathan Goldberg,

Bruce Boehrer, Claude Summers, Ross Leasure and Philip Rollinson (to name only a few). But it seems that each attempt to connect Milton's literary corpus to the concerns and methodologies of queer studies ritualistically reasserts its lonely and embattled status. While describing the suppression of the accusations of buggery of male servants against Mervin Touchet in the Castlehaven scandal (now widely regarded as essential to the background of Milton's "A Masque at Ludlow Castle, 1934" [Comus]), Ross Leasure notes that "such tactics were especially employed when dealing with Touchet's homosexual activities, and may coincide with the general reticence of Miltonists [. . .] to acknowledge anything "queer" in or about the Miltonian canon."[17] Leasure is not alone in feeling so alone.

The constructive scholarly work that has been done has been dominated by redemptive patterns of recovery, of the search for encrypted or lost homosexual meaning in an alternately despairing and affirmative historiographical mode that Heather Love has memorably identified as "emotional rescue."[18] In *Sodomy and Interpretation* Gregory Bredbeck makes the promising claim that Milton's work "suggests a space of meaning outside the heterocentrically prescriptive codes of ideal Renaissance genders,"[19] The most compelling example of this outer space beyond gender normativity occurs in *Paradise Lost*'s account of angelic sexuality, whose ambiguous suggestions of "a life of homosexual promiscuity" prompted dismissive foreclosure of these "filthy" and "foolish" notions from C. S. Lewis in his *Preface to Paradise Lost*. Yet, in a chapter forbiddingly titled "The Mistake About Milton's Angels," Lewis evades the specter of male homosexual angels by recourse to an even queerer formulation of a celestial hermaphroditic free- for-all:

> [. . .] there exists among these creatures, according to Milton, something that might be called trans-sexuality. The impulse of mutual love is expressed by the total interpenetration of two aereal bodies; 'total they mix' because they are ductile and homogenous- they mix like wine and water, or like two wines.[20]

Bredbeck notes that "while the fallen spirits can range freely throughout the system of sex and gender, unfallen spirits can range freely *outside of it*."[21] Yet, frustratingly, having noted this Bredbeck generally sticks to the script of simply discovering or uncovering traces of male homosexuality in the Miltonic text. In response to the willful resistance to homosexual signification prevalent within Milton criticism, Bredbeck seems more interested in the compensatory demonstration that homoerotic meaning was available to Milton within the period courtesy of classical pastoral, and that, in choosing not to assign sodomitical temptation but rather patriarchal temptation to Belial, Milton demonstrated on at least one occasion a willingness to refrain from deploying one available commonplace of anti-sodomy rhetoric. The affirmative cast of such critical quarry is a first step, but one whose lonesome echo calls for a following response which reconsiders the volatility of the a-gendered zones that both Milton's work and Lewis' text potentially make available to the queer critic.

Bredbeck's recovery of the lost non-heteronormative potential of Milton's angels is a tantalizing possibility upstaged by the central importance within his chapter that he grants to a momentary holiday from homophobic abuse in *Paradise Regained*; the real stakes of the project hinge upon the attempt to infer some kind of provisional glimmer of acceptance, or at least recognition of a specifically male homosexual possibility as slightly less than the worst thing that could happen, within the Miltonic corpus. This kind of stance towards the lost or encrypted homosexuality exemplifies what Foucault termed "the consoling play of recognitions" at the core of traditional historical practice in his essay "Nietzsche, Genealogy, History."[22] Bredbeck's introductory scene of the queer theorist righting the homophobic wrongs of past scholarship remains mired in a self-serving rhetoric about gay male visibility that belies the conformist contours of its own structuring imperative as a scene in which the proliferation of "trans-sexual" meanings is replaced by the interpretive production of legibly homosexual, i.e. homo-normative, male subjects.[23]

I want to suggest that if queer readers are to engage Milton's writing otherwise, we should not only hunt for buried, encrypted, or subterranean representations of homosexuality and homoeroticism that are potentially positive or affirmative in character, but also attend more closely to the negative affects of anxiety, shame and hostility generated by moments of queer possibility within these texts, and try to think about how issues of form, monstrosity, racialization, and hybridity inflect the operation of textual "queerness." Instead of hopefully amplifying one solitary instance in which Milton pulls a punch and demurs from attacking sodomy with gusto, one might also want to discuss the far more frequent occasions on which he happily and enthusiastically does exactly that, and to listen more closely to the grain and character of that hostility. These moments of antagonism and hatred for sodomy and effeminacy seem intuitively more consistent with the overall tenor of Milton's religious commitments and rhetorical postures as I read and understand them, and owning up to them in the context of a queer reading might allow us to avoid the "Milton-one-of-us syndrome" that Marshall Grossman has identified as one of the stumbling blocks to appropriationist encounters with Milton that seek to reform or refashion Milton to better resemble contemporary ideals.[24] Such a reorientation seems necessary if we are to provide a productive account of how and where "queerness" surfaces within the Miltonic corpus.

Blind Sodomites and Hybrid Animals

Comprising curiously macho fifteen-year-old female virgins, curiously weepy shaven-headed strongmen, coy trans-sexual angels, thyrsus-wielding Virgilian shepherds, and Puritan propagandists prone to curiously theatrical displays of anti-theatrical ranting, Miltonic queerness is an affective/rhetorical manifold that swings both ways between praise and blame. But it tends towards blame. When it arises in the prose writing, queer meanings and significations produce a choppy linguistic surface of strongly negative repudiation, virulent disgust and comic scorn. Milton's willingness to rhetorically tar his enemies with a sodomitical brush is an old habit born during his first officially sanctioned engagement for the Council of State as Secretary for Foreign Tongues of the interregnum government, *Eikonoklastes* (1649). In the preface to that text, those who praise and dote upon Charles I's defects, because they are his, are said to inhabit a state of "strucken blindness" which borders upon the comparable spiritual blindness of Sodomites:

> That they who from the first beginning or but now of late, by what unhappiness I know not, are so much affatuated not with his person only but with his palpable faults, and dote upon his deformities, may have none to blame but their own folly if they live and die in such a strucken blindness, as next to that of Sodom hath not happened to any sort of men more gross or more misleading.[25]

That sodomites are accused of spiritual blindness is a telling accusation coming from someone in the midst of a battle with literal, physical blindness, and tempts one to hear sadness and fear blending beneath the defensive, hectoring tone. This strategic disavowal of blindness ("it is not I who am blind but you") recurs, of course, in the *Second Defense* in the context of Milton's assault on the royalist's emotional attachment to the legacy of the martyred Charles, an attachment that he repeatedly characterizes as effeminate.[26]

Such shaming recurs throughout the *Second Defense of the English People*, as when he cattily refers to his continental opponent as "Salmasius (or Salmasia, for which of the two he was, the open domination of his wife, both in public and in private, had made it quite difficult to determine)."[27] Writing against Alexander More and Adriaan Vlacq, respectively the supposed author and the publisher of *The Cry of the Royal Blood to Heaven, against the English Parricides*, whose agitated attacks upon both Milton's person constituted the occasion for the *Second Defense*, Milton transfers the accusation from an *ad hominem* attack into a corresponding charge against their writing: "These peddlers of effeminate little verses – who would not despise them?"[28] While such rhetorical assaults are neither surprising given the pamphlet-war context nor particularly unique to Milton, I wish to argue that they are, for all this, more than a passing reflex of vituperation. If, in cocking one's ear to the tone with which the linked accusations of sodomy and effeminacy are thrown at Milton's enemies in the tracts and pamphlets, one hears curiously persistent notes of strangled, encrypted, and disavowed identification, some might object that this only indexes the perverse interpretive reflex engendered by a rote queer studies praxis all too eager to immediately flip expressions of disgust into expressions of covert desire. Such moves can of course seem awfully glib, a kind of queer-positive theoretical variant of the everyday acts of "wild psychoanalysis" committed beneath the shade of a popular psychology giggling to itself about omnipresent "latent homosexuality." Sometimes disgust is just disgust. And yet, Milton's willingness to publicly connect blindness with sodomy in the context of his pamphlet-war combat with his Royalist enemies is simply too fraught with overdetermined layers of identification and disavowal to ignore, precisely because the trope of sodomitical blindness was invoked in the period as a figure for both physically reproductive "errant" desires and for textually (over)productive critical activity.

Admittedly, the counterintuitive assertion that "blind" acts of sodomy must be understood as *reproductive* in a manner that models certain kinds of textual productivity will require some historical explanation and fleshing out. The accusation in *Eikonoklastes* that the men of Sodom suffered from some kind of spiritual "blindness" was indeed a commonplace; what is compelling for my argument is that this specific connection between blindness and sodomy was figured in the prose of the period not (only) in conjunction with homosexuality but with the production of monstrous and chimerical hybrids that were said to be the result of acts of sodomy committed upon animals. Consider the following extended discussion of "a cow that gave birth to a half- man" in Ambroise Paré's teratological tract *On Monsters and Marvels:*

> Now I shall refrain from writing here about several other monsters engendered from such grist, together with their portraits, which are so hideous and abominable, not only to see but also to hear tell of, that, due to their great loathsomeness I have neither wanted to relate them nor have them portrayed. For (as Boistau says, after having related several sacred and profane stories, which are all filled with grievous punishment for lechers) what can atheists and sodomists expect, who (as I said above) couple against God and Nature with brute animals? *On this subject, Saint Augustine says the punishment of lechers is to fall into blindness and to become insane, after they have forsaken God, and not to see their blindness, being unable to follow good counsel.*[29]

Far from being condemned to an unproductive and anality-inflected sterility, the spiritually "blind" sodomite is instead figured as all-too-fertile, creating a hybrid offspring whose unspeakable / unrepresentable loathsomeness in fact energizes and makes possible the very text that struggles to reject it. Unfazed by Paré's strong expressions of personal disgust and stated unwillingness to have such monsters portrayed, the editors of the text accompanied his description of such monstrous births with a suitably bizarre sequence of woodcuts depicting the products of such unions: "Figure of a child, part dog," "Figure of a monster with the face of a man and the body of a goat," "A monster, half-man, half-swine," "Figure of a monster like a dog with the head like a bird," etc.[30] It is here that the *queerness of early modern sodomy* – rather than and indeed, instead of, the homosexuality of early modern sodomy – emerges most forcefully: sodomitical sexuality was imagined in the period as a potentially reproductive sexuality, and its hybrid generativity cannot be thought outside of a subtending racial imaginary which regarded the possibility of such mixtures with fear and fascination.

Dagon as Queer Assemblage

Similarly, while descanting upon the specific quality of his opponent's sodomitical and effeminate deformity, Milton decries their *literary* production as a monstrous hybrid in a manner that reminds one of Paré's medical catalogues of hybrid monsters. Consider this mockery of More and Vlaacq in the *Second Defense* in terms of Paré's beast-fable of sodomitical creation:

> But listen! Another Cry, something strange and hissing. I take it that geese are flying in from somewhere or other. Now I realize what it is. I remember that this is the Tragedy of a Cry. The Chorus appears. Behold two poetasters – either two or a single one, twofold in appearance and of two colors. Should I call it a sphinx, or that monster which Horace described in the *Ars Poetica*, with the head of a woman, the neck of an ass, clad in varied plumage, with limbs assembled from every source? Yes, this is that very monster.[31]

Far from a stereotypical overspill of a liquid femininity into the solid terrain of masculine psychic life, the monstrous sodomitical construction of royalist writing requires a new morphological imaginary that solders together component parts sourced across gender *and* species barriers and stapled together seemingly by chance.[32] The mongrel nature of these creations mirrors the mongrel nature of their creators, and the royalist authors are themselves understood as aggregates of components: in a paratactic and inclusive jumbling of linked but separate pejorative senses that calls to mind Polonius' "tragical-comical-historical-pastoral," Milton's opponents are censured for presenting the public with the blind-sodomitical-hybrid- effeminate-theatrical.

In evoking the monstrosity of a creature "with limbs assembled from every source" taken out of Horace, Milton here refers to the lines which begin the famous "Letter to Piso," which I provide here in Ben Jonson's translation as "Horace, of the Art of Poetry":

> If to a woman's head a painter would
> Set a horse-neck, and diverse feathers fold
> On every limb, ta'en from a severall creature,
> Presenting upwards a fair female feature.
> Which in some swarthy fish uncomely ends:
> Admitted to the sight, although his friends,
> Could you contain your laughter?[33]

In contrast with this painted image, great poetry ought to "Be simple, quite throughout, and wholly one." By yoking together human and animal elements and miscegenating the "fair" and the "swarthy" into an uncomely new (anti)form, the painter's work fails to achieve synthesis and verisimilitude, stalling instead at the level of collage with a one-man *cadavre exquis*. Yet the very priority of this assemblage, coming as it does at the head of an extended discussion of compositional strategy, lends a curious kind of exemplarity and mystique to this icon of the ridiculous; indeed the incident itself feels appended like an extraneous head onto the rambling text that follows it, tainting the compositional lecture itself with an associative formal resemblance to the chimerical anecdote that begins it. Furthermore, one might want to attend to the private unveiling of this image as a gendered scene, in which the homosocial sodality of male artist and his friends gather together to regard a painted image of a female body gone awry. The inability to correctly fashion an imaginary woman marks the painter with a double lack: a lapse in artistic skill that may also signal a failure of sexual maturity and savoir-faire. One has failed as a man and as a painter if one does not know how to "make" a woman. Further complicating this humorous scene, racial anxiety compounds and reinforces gender monstrosity. The mixture of the human and the inhuman and the mixture of the "fair" and the "swarthy" presents human- animal hybrids and racially mixed hybrids as if it were already intuitively obvious that they figure each other, thus reifying the subordinate inhumanity of "swarthy" races as a naturalized reflection of the species barrier among animals while replacing the frightening possibility of the biological viability of interracial mixtures with a comically "impossible" gallimaufry of scraps.

One way to measure the distance between Horatian poetics and their early modern recurrence is precisely in the shifting position of such assemblages along the spectrum between praise and blame. Far from functioning transparently as a self-evident example of the failure of the poet to observe the laws of representational decorum, by the sixteenth century the construction of such chimerical assemblages came to be daringly identified with the very essence of the poetic act, now redefined as a prosthetic extension of the natural into "a new nature." The phrase comes from Sir Philip Sidney's *Defence of Poetry* (1595), in which the quasi-magical capacity of the poet to re-form nature is invoked in reference to the deliberate construction of the unnatural: "Only the poet, disdaining to be tied to any such subjection, lifted up with the vigor of his own invention, doth grow in effect another nature, in making things either better than nature bringeth forth, or, quite anew, forms such as never were in nature, as the Heroes, Demigods, Cyclops, Chimeras, Furies, and such like."[34] If this repertoire of new creations is resolutely classical, the assertion of the dignity of artificiality sounds a distinctly un-Horatian note, but also admits directly the possibility of the chimerical assemblage as a desired object, as something not only monstrous but also intoxicating, fascinating.

Such a possibility is consciously kept under wraps in Milton's prose. For Milton, at least in the heated moment of rhetorical battle, the compositional failure involved in fashioning such a "very monster" reflects back upon the failed genders of their creators in a manner calculated to revive the censorious critical laughter that Horace also sought to inspire. The effeminacy of More and Vlaacq, their status as men somehow mixed with and compromised by a contemptible surplus of femininity, is mirrored in the formal admixtures of their literary creations: they, like their writing, are hybrids, chimerical assemblages, equally comical and repellent. But the Horatian background to Milton's passing swipe also signals a more important connection between the gendered rhetoric of his prose and the imaginative substratum of his poetry. The Horatian monstrosity is not only part female, but *part fish*, and this specific woman/fish assemblage recurs in a telling (and also partially submerged) manner in Milton's representation of Dagon, the Philistine deity whose festival triggers Samson's cataclysmic outburst of divine violence in *Samson Agonistes*.

Dagon as Queer Assemblage

Reappearing at every stage of his poetic development, the image of Dagon's violated, inhuman form seems to enjoy the status of an idée fixe in Milton's literary imagination. Dagon initially appears in "On the Morning of Christ's Nativity," in Milton's first catalog of pagan divinities bewailing the birth of the Savior, as an epithet of abuse rather than a proper name: "Peor and Baalim, / Forsake their temples dim, / With that twice-battered god of Palestine." (lines 197-199) When Dagon returns in the catalog of pagan gods and "gay religions of pomp and gold" in Book I of *Paradise Lost*, Milton's describes in detail this "twice battered" Palestinian body's progress from hybrid formation to humbling mutilation:

> Next came one
> Who mourned in earnest, when the captive ark
> Maimed his brute image, head and hands lopped off
> In his own temple, on the grunsel edge,
> Where he fell flat, and shamed his worshippers:
> Dagon his name, sea monster, upward man
> And downward fish: yet had his temple high
> Reared in Azotus, dreaded through the coast
> Of Palestine, in Gath and Ascalon
> And Accaron and Gaza's frontier bounds. (457-466)

The recent Kerrigan, Rumrich and Fallon edition points out that "'Dag' is Hebrew for fish" but does not further clarify that Dagon's fishy provenance is the result of a false etymological slippage between the original Ugaritic root word for grain ("dgn") and its Hebrew near- homonym.[35] For our purposes this misprision need not detain us, as Milton's understanding of Dagon is derived entirely from the Hebrew text of 1. Samuel 5.1-7, which describes the Philistine captivity of the ark and the humiliating outcome of a combat between the Ark of the Covenant and the idol of Dagon. In the *Geneva Bible* (1560) the passage reads as follows:

> Then the Philistims toke the Arke of God and caryed it from Eben-ezer unto Ashdod, Evn the Philistims toke the Arke of God, and broght it into the house of Dagon, and set it by Dagon. And they of Ashdod rose the next day in the morning, beholde, Dagon was fallen upon his face on the

> ground before the Arke of the Lord, and they toke up Dagon, and set him in his place againe. Also they rose up early in the morning the next day, & beholde, Dagon was falle upon his face on the grounde before the Arke of the Lord, and the head of Dagon and the two palmes of his hands were cut off upon the thresholde: onely the stumpe of Dagon was left to him. (I. Samuel 5.1-4)

Period Biblical scholarship rendered the latent "meaning" in Dagon's name explicit in marginal commentary on this passage; the Geneva Bible glosses this tale with a note that Dagon "was their chiefe idole, & as some write, from ye [. . .] downward like a fishe, and upwarde like a man." (I. Samuel.5.2), a description directly echoed, but poetically corrected, in Milton's epic, which tumbles across the linebreak to formally enact the split in his morphology: "Dagon his name, sea monster, upward man / And downward fish." (462-463)[36] But Milton's sequential descent from higher humanity to lower animality also, of course, summons in the mind of the reader the half- conscious internal expectation of a term more frequently held in opposition to the dominant term of "man," namely, woman. From the waist up Dagon may be all man, but the fishy nether regions swim with alternate morphological possibilities.

I do not mean to suggest that Dagon is "really" female in any clear sense; indeed, to do so would be to shut down the liquidity of Dagon's oceanic associations and to misrepresent the manifold nature of how Milton understands divine form. In its capacity to slip free of the intransigent weight of the merely sexed human, Dagon's underlayer of hermaphroditic meanings partakes of the material ambiguity attendant upon not only embryonic potential humans but all spirits, both angelic and demonic:

> For spirits when they please
> Can either sex assume, or both; so soft
> And uncompounded is their essence pure,
> Nor tied or manacled with joint or limb,
> Nor founded on the brittle strength of bones,
> Like cumbrous flesh; but in what shape they choose
> Dilated or condensed, bright or obscure,
> Can execute their airy purposes
> And works of love or enmity fulfill. (423-431)

Noting such choice and flexibility only takes us so far, however, and in the case of Dagon it ignores the brute fact of idolatry's fixation not on an airy spirit but on an object that can be mutilated or knocked down. The tale in Samuel of the prostration of Dagon's idol before the Ark, and of the subsequent decapitation of the idol resolutely materializes Dagon into a massive, thingy affront to the primacy of the god of Israel.

Dagon's abased and mutilated status in the text of Samuel (first forced to bow down to the Ark, then decapitated and symbolically "circumcised" by the skinning of the palms of both hands) irrevocably marks this divine body as a key site through which to think about the anxiety generated by difference: the tribal conflict between the Philistines and the Israelites plays itself out in a violent script about the failure of idolatry that nonetheless resorts to its figurative logic. Dagon's subordination to the Ark is a battle between two idols, and the text's sadistic imperative to wound or insult the idol of Dagon at some level perpetuates the very thing the story is meant to disprove (idols are powerful, and the need to physically chasten Dagon's idol pays perverse complement to its totemic authority and representational fitness as a tribal protector). Marking and maiming the idol of the enemy expresses a rage to differentiate that encrypts an anxious sense of proximity; it is not safe to set Dagon and the Ark beside each other. If Dagon's body is marked in its appearance in *Paradise Lost* as irrevocably wounded by its encounter with the absolute sovereignty of the Ark, Dagon in *Samson Agonistes* telescopes backwards before this event from Samuel to Judges, and represents idolatry ascendant, a chiasmic popular embodiment of both the error of monstrosity and the monstrosity of error.

Forecasting and inverting this conflict, Manoa's shaming speech to his son constitutes a kind of traumatic alternative to the text of Samuel, a fearful scenario in which the God of Israel is brought low by Dagon ascendant:

> This day the Philistines a popular feast
> Here celebrate in Gaza, and proclaim
> Great pomp, and sacrifice, and praises loud
> To Dagon, as their god who hath delivered
> Thee Samson bound and blind into their hands,
> Them out of thine, who slew'st them many a slain.
> So Dagon shall be magnified, and God,
> Besides whom is no God, compared with idols,
> Disglorified, blasphemed, and had in scorn
> By th'idolatrous rout amidst their wine. (434-443)

We can now see why Samson's self-hatred and Samson's hatred of Dagon are mutually supportive: his effeminate subjection to Dalila has produced the God of Israel's idolatrous subjection to Dagon. The idol's hybridity as a man/fish (woman) assemblage shamefully signifies Samson's exogamous desires, embodying in a grotesquely literal manner the "mixture with the other" that has effeminately subjected the Nazarite hero to a foreign woman. Neither fish nor flesh, Dagon's mixed status recalls the shame brought down upon his head by Samson's own exogamous wanderings from his people in favor of sexual alliances with ethnically (racially?) distinct women, first with the nameless "woman of Timna" and then with Dalila. To put it baldly, so to speak, Samson's shame arises as a result of his sexual preference. His status as the deliverer and judge of his people has been compromised by his desire to stray from them into bed with Canaanites and Philistines.

Seen from different angles, Dagon represents both Samson and Dalila, and this mutual figuration furthers the play of resemblance within the text as "manliness" encounters itself in its others. As a strange woman and her strange god, Dalila and Dagon are made to subtly stand in for each other in a revealing, if comic, moment in *Samson Agonistes* when the chorus describes the approach of an ambiguous figure to the blind hero: "But who is this, what thing of sea or land? / Female of sex it seems" (710-711) The chorus' confusion about this mysterious entity from either sea or land has been taken to be a mockery of Aristotelian disquisition and progressively finer distinctions, but it also seems richly resonant with Dagon's chimerical status as an idolatrous "thing" composed of elements from both "sea" and "land." Dalila's mysterious apparition to the chorus hovers between the borders policed by the anti-idolatrous injunction of Exodus 20.4. ("You shall not make for yourself an idol, whether in the form of anything that is in heaven above, or that is on the earth beneath, or that is in the water under the earth.") In elevating his romantic allegiance to Dalila above his duties as a Nazarite to Israel, Samson in effect has committed a kind of romantic/sexual idolatry in choosing her that the poetic drama works to repudiate and correct. If Dalila only "seems" to be of female sex, this certainly calls the chorus' own visual acuity into question, fingering them as "blind guides" to Samson who only just see better than the blind slave they counsel, but it also further amplifies the queerness of the Dalila/Dagon pair, suggesting that there is something misleading or astray about their very gender, something either in disguise or permanently in the process of becoming. In the wake of her final salvo to Samson, Dalila becomes an animal: "She's gone, a manifest serpent by her sting / Discovered in the end, till now concealed." (997-998) In this final act of "becoming animal" she shares a fate with Samson's posthumous choral description, which is, is Julia Lupton's fine phrase, "a veritable eruption of animalia."[37] Figuring him first as a Dragon, and then as an Eagle, Samson's aura of monstrous power and brute inhumanity are subjected to a final torque of gender and species re-assignment when the chorus compares his final resurgence of divine strength with the resurrection of the female Phoenix from her own "ashy womb" (1697-1705).

Samson as "Terrorist Look-Alike" and Dagon Look-Alike

Less than kin and more than kind, "anxiety" and "terror" occupy a usefully disjunctive proximity to each other in critical work on affect, and since I have slid between these two terms in order to think about Samson's anxiety and his acts of terror as a linked pair, I had better explain why. As Sianne Ngai has usefully sketched in the introduction to her chapter on anxiety in *Ugly Feelings*, anxiety is both omnipresent and under-theorized, particularly in psychoanalysis, where, in an account less than fully cashed out by Freud, it is suggestively if fleetingly described as the projected displacement onto others of a trait disavowed yet discovered in the self.[38] Described by Ernst Bloch as an "expectant emotion" that "opens out entirely [into the] horizon of time," anxiety manifests its distorting effects in the present on behalf of a dreadful, imminent futurity, a potentiality held always in reserve.[39] By contrast, to rise from "mere" anxiety to the exalted and heightened affective state of genuine "terror" would seem to require some kind of direct encounter with the threatening presence/existence of the object-cause of fear; terror, to be legitimate, needs some kind of proof or objective ratification, and here Ngai's attention to the "ignoble" strains of affect usefully flags the problematic comparative "weakness" of anxiety in comparison with its grandiose neighbor, terror.[40] Insofar as terror is terror "at" something and anxiety is a projection "from" the self, the two would seem to just miss each other, falling on either side of some hoary boundaries that we theorists are said to do without: public/private, self/other.

But the overlapping yet distinct states of terror and anxiety can feed and sustain each other: Within the rhetorical self-understanding of the ongoing "war on terror" that characterizes both government policy and public discourse in the United States, the wrenching, confirming experience of terrorist violence "proves" that our sources of terror have an external cause in this world whose potential future resurgence verifies and legitimates an ongoing, endless vigilance whose signature affect is a slow burn of omnipresent anxiety. Anxiety stands in for but also draws its support from the enabling fact of "terror," closing a feedback loop anchored at both ends of a temporal horizon: the terror of "then" sanctions the anxiety of "now" on behalf of an endlessly expected return of a terror "to come."

Working through the intersection of these terms, I think we can overlay the temporal/social structure of displacement at the core of theories of anxiety onto the dramatic structure of *Samson Agonistes*, allowing us to think about Samson's final act of destructive religious violence (an act of "terror") as a violent ratification and expulsive expression of an ongoing emotional state (his nonstop "act" – in the sense of public affective display – of anxiety). Releasing anxiety into terror, the destruction of the feast of Dagon is the triumphant terrorist catastrophe that retroactively justifies and releases the affect stored/savored/suffered as anxiety across Milton's notoriously static, staunchly talky exercise in Senecan closet-drama. Framed thusly, that very dramatic structure's problematic resemblance to narrative arcs at work in the ongoing "war on Terror," a context through which Milton's text is increasingly read, redoubles this problem of anxiety as the refusal of a resemblance (or, really, the terrifying grip of the fearful recognition of a resemblance). In particular, I think we can read recent expenditures of critical energy dedicating to preventing terrorist meaning from attaching to Milton as themselves an ongoing work of anxious displacement.

This is particularly the case with the pressure that the Carey/Fish debate continues to exert upon the scene of Milton interpretation. Acknowledgement of the "debate" is mandatory, if the introductory comments included in recent critical editions of Milton are taken as evidence. Stoking the flames in a contest of ever more indignant and anxious defenses of Milton/Fish (it is occasionally hard to tell the difference in the more partisan accounts) from these charges, the recent anthology *Milton in the Age of Fish: Essays on Authorship, Text, and Terrorism* collects together a range of responses to the controversy, including, naturally, a quintessentially barbed and bemused contribution from Fish himself.

To reduce things down to proper size, the dispute hinges upon debates about the fitness of Carey's account of Fish's account of Milton's account of

Samson's understanding of a divine message from God that sanctions the violent destruction of the feast of Dagon. In a usefully skeptical assessment of the entire exchange, Feisal G. Mohammed notes the subterranean consensus that organizes this mutually convenient display of polemical pyrotechnics on both the (lonely) Carey side and in the (overpopulated) Fish camp. Each side works to protect Milton from openly advocating a "terrorist" meaning. Having parsed Fish's reading as one which leads us to the uncomfortable conclusion that Milton gives us no way to discredit the "great act" that Samson commits, Carey's most inflammatory statements are interrogatives: if this is what *Samson Agonistes* itself advocates, "should [the work] not be withdrawn from schools and colleges and, indeed, banned more generally as an incitement to terrorism?"[41] These calls are designed to prompt a solidly humanist "surely not" from the *TLS* congregation, and manifest Carey's faith that Milton must be critiquing religious violence and urging us to read Samson's "rousing inward motions" that prompt his destruction of the temple of Dagon critically and ironically.[42]

Demurring from common ground, the Fish contingent respond that the problem of how to evaluate Samson's violence is the point of the poem, alleging that we cannot know whether or not Milton condemns Samson because we cannot know whether the "rousing inward motions" that Samson feels do indeed come from God or not.[43] The dispute stalls at the limits of what we can know about "the interior recesses of the willing and intending heart."[44] There is, I think, a curious queer echo here. Try reading the following account of Samson's motivations with a queer inflection: "Only the intention, the unbidden and constitutive inward orientation, makes the difference, and the difference can only be recognized by one who is its (internal) bearer. *It takes one to know one.*"[45] Fish is talking about how to tell a terrorist from a religiously inspired hero, but his language of "willing hearts" and "unbidden orientations" suggests an altogether queerer register of intersubjective speculation. Reading the anxiety generated by the threat of effeminacy "within" (in every sense) Samson alongside the critical anxiety generated by the threat of terrorist meaning within Milton's text, a shared logic of displacement produces a formal structure in which an inaccessible abyss of interiority is posited as a bar to knowing/seeing. Effeminacy on the plane of gender and terrorism on the plane of religious politics occupy a shared structural position as the excluded-yet-ineradicable perverse possibility that mobilizes and justifies a violent and repressive response within the text and in the persistent patterns of critical denial outside and about it.[46]

I hope I have not been struggling by oblique or critically paranoid means to say that there is some proto-, crypto-, demi-, quasi-, or pseudo-homosexual subject buried "within" the encrypted inwardness of Samson's "rousing inward motions," nor am I suggesting that his repeated bewailing of his effeminacy constitutes some repudiation of an "inner" homosexual subjectivity.[47] Patently, Samson's anxiety about his effeminacy is not hidden, repressed or concealed; it's there on the page before us, and present in his mouth as he bewails its "foul embrace" to anyone who will listen. What is displaced, disavowed, or refused by Samson is a feeling of proximity or resemblance between himself and the creaturely hybridity of Dagon, a feeling that collects as anxiety and explodes into terror. With this dynamic in mind, let us now return to Lupton's formulation with which I began: "Milton's Samson is finally not typological (a figure of Christ), or even typological in a terminally suspended way ("exil'd from light"), but *anti-typological*, arresting the recuperative moment of typology in the sheer violence of his act."[48] The title of Lupton's essay, "Samson Dagonistes," elegantly weds two elements that I have joined together, with far less elegance, as a "queer assemblage," and I owe much of my own understanding of how to think about the politics and poetics of Milton's writing to her example. But here I want to suggest that the violent resistance to the hold or claim of typology within Samson that Lupton detects might be directed not forward to Christian appropriations and equivalences but "backwards," to the forces of chthonic and pagan idolatry that press up against his blind, subjected, "effeminated" Nazarite body. The resemblance being violently rejected is not a resemblance between Samson and Christ but rather the resemblance between Samson and Dagon, the typological equivalence that Lupton's very title proposes, in which the sidelong axis of comparison and competition (which will later produce the decisive conflict between God and Dagon in 1 Samuel) screens out the backwards/inwards pressure of effeminacy within and the terrifying, terror-producing pressures of racial/sexual/ethnic/species-based otherness without.

Chimerical Conclusion

The notion of an "assemblage" need not, in and of itself, arrive fraught with terrifying implications: if Dagon is an inter-species assemblage, so is a chicken and bacon sandwich. Yet the chimerical hybrid body remains threatening, and threateningly present all the same, and not only in the terrorist register that Jasbir Puar has theorized; as hasty legislation and corporate bioethical policy boards struggle to catch up with the accelerating pace of genetic engineering, our own historical moment is one of the nonstop proliferation of biological chimeras, hybrids, mashups, "queer assemblages" across national borders and species barriers.[49] In a passage from "Nietzsche, Genealogy, History" that has become something of a touchstone for queer theory, Michel Foucault wrote that: "History becomes 'effective' to the degree that it introduces discontinuity into our very being–as it divides our emotions, dramatizes our instincts, multiplies our body and sets it against itself."[50] Surveying the ruined panorama of the present, it is not hard to find discontinuities in our being, divided emotions, instinctual dramas, multiplied bodies, and states divided against themselves. Indeed, it's hard *not* to find them. One might point to the way that Craigslist murders compete with transatlantic bombers, embryonic rabbit-human fusions, pigs whose hearts beat with human blood, and instantly uplinked cell phone footage of bombed funerals, bombed weddings, executed tyrants and decapitated journalists for the morcellated remains of our attention – were it not for the sad certainty that nothing dates faster than the contemporary indexes of our own supposedly irreversible freefall into fragmentation. If (and this is a genuine if) the trans-historical acts of recognition that queer studies have up to now provided have helped us to understand the desires, pleasures, and terrors of bodies past, there is no standing guarantee that these logics – of assemblage, of anxiety – will continue to address the divided and discontinuous bodies of today. Foucault told us that "the genealogist needs history to dispel the chimeras of the origin."[51] What resources do we need in order to converse with the chimeras of the present?

Notes

1. John Carey, "A Work in Praise of Terrorism? September 11 and *Samson Agonistes*," *Times Literary Supplement*. September 6, 2002. 15-16.
2. Unless otherwise noted, all references to Milton's poetry are taken from *The Complete Poetry and Essential Prose of John Milton*, eds. William Kerrigan, John Rumrich, and Stephen M. Fallon (New York: Modern Library, 2007). All prose works are quoted from the relevant volume of *The Complete Prose Works of John Milton*, eds. Robert Ayers and Austin Woolrych (New Haven: Yale University Press, 1953-82).
3. Julia Reinhard Lupton, "Samson Dagonistes," in *Citizen-Saints: Shakespeare and Political Theology* (Chicago: University of Chicago Press, 2005) 181-205, 202.
4. As Amanda Bailey has noted, "The word 'masculinity', which did not enter the English language until the middle of the eighteenth century, referred to the privilege awarded to men in matters of inheritance. 'Manhood' and 'manliness' were the terms used in the sixteenth century to connote those qualities essential to civility, which was identified teleologically as the definitive characteristic of the adult man." Amanda Bailey, *Flaunting: Style and the Subversive Male Body in Renaissance England* (Toronto: University of Toronto Press, 2007), 48.
5. The "yoke" invoked in the phrase "the yoke of foul effeminacy" is itself a kind of rhetorical switchpoint. Here it figures not simply the subjection of man to woman, hence a reversal of the expected hierarchical power relations within marriage, but also the yoking of manhood to effeminacy. This "misyoking marriage" is a grotesque inversion of the positive ways in which marital submission is depicted as a just expression of manly self-discipline in the divorce tracts, as when Milton alleges that if Parliament wisely permits divorce to justly dissatisfied husbands, then "the yoke of prudent and manly discipline will be generally submitted to." Milton, *The Doctrine and Discipline of Divorce*, 863.
6. OED, italics mine.
7. David M. Halperin, *How to Do the History of Homosexuality* (Chicago: University of Chicago Press, 2002), 33.
8. I do not mean to suggest that this reading of the "One-Sex Model" hegemonically determines the current state of early modern scholarship about gender. The overly rigid application of this model has been challenged on both dramatic grounds and on medico-historical grounds from several directions; see Janet Adelman's essay "Making Defect Perfection: Shakespeare and the One-Sex Model," in *Enacting Gender on the English Renaissance Stage*, eds. Viviana Comensoli and Anne Russell (Urbana: University of Illinois Press, 1999), 23-52, for an alternative to the Laqueur/Greenblatt formulation.
9. These terms were first used in a series of articles for *Social Text*, and are now collected together, sometimes in revised forms, in Jasbir Puar, *Terrorist Assemblages: Homonationalism in Queer Times* (Durham: Duke University Press, 2007). All Puar quotes are from that text unless otherwise indicated. As a critical and philosophical term of art, "assemblage" is the joint coinage of Gilles Deleuze and Felix Guattari, and denotes a formation of sub-components with expressive consistency but no essence. As such, assemblages range up and down the scale of ontological organization, from molecules to symptoms to cities. Gilles Deleuze and Feliz Guattari, *A Thousand Plateaus: Capitalism and Schizophrenia*, trans. Brian Massumi (Minneapolis: University of Minnesota

Press, 1987). See also Manuel DeLanda, *A New Philosophy of Society: Assemblage Theory and Social Complexity* (London: Continuum, 2006).

    10. Puar, *Terrorist Assemblages*, 54.

    11. Jasbir Puar, "Queer Times, Queer Assemblages," *Social Text* 23.3-4 (Fall-Winter 2005): 121-39, 133.

    12. Puar, *Terrorist Assemblages*, 10.

    13. Puar, *Terrorist Assemblages*, 10.

    14. As Julia Lupton puts it in her essay "Samson Dagonistes," "Samson's final act [. . .] mounts an assault on the very possibility of a public sphere (free assembly and congregation being the true target of terrorism)" (197).

    15. A historical claim about a change in the discursive codes and logics of sexual *prohibition* was recast into a nominalist claim about persons and experience, and the result was the act/identity debate of the 1990s. For a refutation of the widespread misreading of Foucault, see David Halperin's chapter "Forgetting Foucault" in *How to Do the History of Homosexuality*, 24-47. Kenneth Borris' *Same-Sex Desire in the English Renaissance: A Sourcebook of Sixteenth to Mid-Seventeenth Century Texts, 1460-1650* (New York: Routledge, 2004) re-opened the moribund act/identity debate, archivally challenging the de facto persistence of the "acts paradigm" by restoring to view a culturally available early modern notion of same-sex-desiring subjects. Carla Freccero's *Queer / Early / Modern* (Durham: Duke University Press, 2006) complicates – but does not counter – Borris' work of historical reclamation with a theoretical project designed to frame "queerness" as a ghostly agent that dissolves temporality itself, queering the very act of trans-historical interpretation, and raising the stakes of what we as critics take ourselves to be doing when we "queer the Renaissance."

    16. The key works on this topic that still largely dominate the discussion are James Grantham Turner's *One Flesh: Paradisal Marriage and Sexual Relations in the Age of Milton* (Oxford: Oxford University Press, 1987); and Joseph Wittreich's *Feminist Milton* (Ithaca: Cornell University Press, 1987). For a more recent scholarly collection of work on the topic, see Catherine Gimelli Martin, ed., *Milton and Gender* (Cambridge: Cambridge University Press, 2004).

    17. Ross Leasure, "Milton's Queer Choice: Comus at Castlehaven," *Milton Quarterly* 36 (2002): 63-86, 78. Reticence is a kind way to put it. The largely inhospitable climate of Milton studies to such considerations might be conveyed in a telling if perhaps unfair quotation from an essay by Diane Kelsey McColley entitled "Milton and the Sexes" that graces *The Cambridge Companion to Milton*, ed. Dennis Danielson (Cambridge: Cambridge University Press, 1999): "Curiously, some people object to Eve's derivation from Adam, in spite of her original splendour in truth, beauty, wisdom and sanctitude, who are unalarmed by the news that we are all derived from hairy bipeds called *Australopithecus afarensis*. Some resent her service to 'God in him' who recommend the narrower confines of 'self-servience' and have no interest in service of God at all. Some censure the slight imparity of perfections of Eve and Adam without lamenting our general inferiority to them both. Some think Eve unfree who do not protest the massive oppression of psychological theories that put each person and all action and affection into a few sexual categories and locate the genesis of all creativity in the vicinity of that portion of the male body on which 'Adam sat'" (163). And so on. There is indeed much that is "curious" about this situation, from McColley's evocation of the evolution- endorsing, Freud-besotted, godless horde to the torturous discretion she marshals when prodded to indicate the precise vicinity of the anus. Granting that McColley's rhetorical intention is to estrange beliefs she assumes are normative in her readership in order hopefully to warm them to the possibility that Milton's religious convictions are no more ridiculous than their evolutionary or psychoanalytic explanatory frameworks, such jeremiads have the de facto effect of evangelizing for the beauty and integrity of those convictions instead of critically unpacking them. Perhaps such defensive displays derive from the sense that, in the wake of T. S. Eliot's right hook and "second wave" feminism's left hook, Milton still needs to be protected from philistine readers (or worse, Milton's readership needs to be whittled back down to a "fit audience, though few"). If this is the predominant tone in Milton studies when it considers some rather old critical frameworks for thinking about sex, sexuality, and gender, then the reluctance of recent queer scholars to even bother entering the fray is hardly surprising. Happily, "Milton studies" accommodates multiple perspectives, as contributions from Gordon Teskey, Julia

Lupton, Ross Leasure, Marshall Grossman, Victoria Kahn and Derek Wood (among many others one might include) amply demonstrate.

18. Heather Love, *Feeling Backward: Loss and the Politics of Queer History* (Cambridge; Harvard University Press, 2007), 51.

19. Gregory Bredbeck, *Sodomy and Interpretation: Marlowe to Milton* (Ithaca: Cornell University Press, 1991), 226. From an unlikely quarter, one can see support for Bredbeck's assertion in Stanley Fish's local recognition of the reversal of gender roles at work in the dialogue between Comus and the Lady. (Stanley Fish, *How Milton Works* [Cambridge: Harvard University Press, 2001], 172). For a full-dress analysis of the gendered implications of Miltonic identification with the Lady, see William Shullenberger's "Milton's Lady and Lady Milton: Chastity, Prophecy and Gender in A Maske Presented at Ludlow Castle," in *Fault Lines and Controversies in the Study of Seventeenth- Century English Literature*, ed. Claude Summers (Columbia: University of Missouri Press, 2002), 204-26.

20. C. S. Lewis, *A Preface to Paradise Lost* (Oxford: Oxford University Press, 1961), 113.

21. Bredbeck, *Sodomy and Interpretation*, 226.

22. Michel Foucault, "Nietzsche, Genealogy, History," in *Language, Counter-Memory, Practice: Selected Essays and Interviews*, trans. Donald F. Bouchard and Sherry Simon (Ithaca: Cornell University Press, 1977), 153.

23. From any perspective, Lewis's *Preface* seems an odd choice as an exemplar of relentlessly straight critical performativity; space prevents a full exegesis, but one might at least arch an eyebrow in passing at the passionate conclusion of Lewis' dedication of his text to the Milton scholar Charles Williams: "Apparently the door of the prison was really unlocked all the time; but it was only you who thought of trying the handle. *Now we can all come out.*" (vi, italics mine). Such overspills of homosocial scholarly affect abound in the archive of the old scholarship against which "out" queer work defines itself, and "trans-sexuality" clearly mattered enough to Lewis for him to import the concept directly into the homosocial milieu of the scholarly male friendship networks he fictionalized in his adult science fiction novel *Perelandra*, where the philologist hero Ransom returns from his expedition to Venus muttering about the "trans-sexuality" of the "eldila," an angelic race of super-beings. C. S. Lewis, *Perelandra* (New York: Scribner, 1944), 30.

24. Marshall Grossman, "The Onomastic Destiny of Stanley Fish," in Michael Lieb and Albert Labriola, eds., *Milton in the Age of Fish: Essays on Authorship, Text, and Terrorism* (Pittsburgh: Duquesne University Press, 2007), 18. Film savvy readers will of course have noted that the chant "one of us, one of us" derives from Todd Browning's 1932 film "Freaks," which, as Grossman notes, concludes with a monstrous transformation of its anti-heroine Cleopatra from a "normal" trapeze artist into a "half woman, half chicken [. . .] put on display in a sideshow" (51). It is entirely in keeping with the Milton's hybrid morphology of difference that a contemporary critic's figure for a Milton who resembles "us" here produces the comic/horrific construction of a monstrous hybrid, built not out of different species but out of anachronistically incommensurable "values."

25. Milton, *The Complete Prose Works*, 1061.

26. For more on the rhetoric of effeminacy and gender in the political tracts and pamphlets, see Gina Hausknecht's essay "The Gender of Civic Virtue," in *Milton and Gender*, ed. Martin, 19-33.

27. Milton, *The Complete Prose Works*, 1077.

28. Milton, *The Complete Prose Works*, 1085.

29. Ambroise Paré, *On Monsters and Marvels*, trans. Janis L. Pallister (Chicago: University of Chicago Press, 1982), 73, italics mine.

30. Paré, 68-71.

31. Milton, *The Complete Prose Works*, 1085.

32. At once pictorial and theatrical, the *Cry* is a monstrous hybrid of persons, genders, species, "colors," and materials. The association of the royalist cause with a maudlin, overwrought and hence risible form of theatricality, implicit in his mockery of "the Tragedy of a Cry," follows from Milton's dismissal of William Marshall's notorious depiction of Charles I that graced *Eikon Basilike*; Milton described it as "the conceited portraiture before his book, *drawn out to the full measure of a masking scene*" (1062, italics mine) Victoria Kahn has noted Milton's response to Marshall's drawing and to the royalist propaganda that surrounded as a critical refusal of the psychology of

pity in favor of "the unsentimental application of justice," but Kahn is less concerned with the explicit gendering of sentimentality. See Victoria Kahn, "Aesthetics as Critique: Tragedy and *Trauerspiel* in *Samson Agonistes*." *Reading Renaissance Ethics*, ed. Marshall Grossman (New York: Routledge, 2007), 104-29, 105.

33. Ben Jonson, "Horace, of the Art of Poetry," *The Complete Poems*, ed. George Parfitt, (London: Penguin Books, 1975), 354-371, 354.

34. Sir Philip Sidney, "A Defence of Poetry" (1595), in *English Renaissance Literary Criticism*, ed. Brian Vickers (Oxford: Clarendon Press, 1999), 336-392, 343.

35. See Milton, *The Complete Poetry and Essential Prose*, 310. For an account of the confusion generated by this name, see Joseph Fontenrose. "Dagon and El" *Oriens* 10.2 (1957): 277-79.

36. Milton loves this trick, which has its debut in an account of another group of animal/human hybrids, the "monsters" engendered by the enchanted liquid in Circe's magic cup: "Whoever tasted, lost his upright shape / And downward fell into a groveling swine." (Milton, "A Masque Presented at Ludlow Castle, 1634" [Comus], lines 52- 53). Unlike his Homeric source, in Milton's version of Comus' acts of transmogrification, only the head of the enchanted person is transformed, thus producing another cross-species assemblage. As described in his stage directions, Comus enters "*with his rout of monsters headed like sundry sorts of wild beasts, but otherwise like men and women.*" (Milton, "A Masque Presented at Ludlow Castle, 1634," 67).

37. Lupton, "Samson Dagonistes," 199.

38. Sianne Ngai, *Ugly Feelings* (Cambridge: Harvard University Press, 2007), 203. Lacan admits as much in his introductory remarks to his seminar on anxiety of 1962-63: "There is no subject where the net of the Freudian discourse is closer, in short, to giving us a false sense of security; because precisely, when we go into this text [Freud's 'Inhibitions, symptoms, and anxiety'] you will see what is to be seen in connection with anxiety, that there is no net, because precisely as regards anxiety, each mesh, as I might appropriately put it, has no meaning except by leaving the void in which anxiety is. In the discourse, thank God, of 'Inhibitions, symptoms, and anxiety,' *everything is spoken about except anxiety*. (Jacques Lacan, *The Seminar of Jacques Lacan: Anxiety 1962 - 1963, Book X*, trans. Cormac Gallgher [Eastbourne, Antony Rowe, 1995], 6, italics mine.) Lacan explicitly defines anxiety as an affect (rather than an emotion) which is not, itself, subject to repression: "One finds it displaced, mad, inverted, metabolized, but it is not repressed. What is repressed are the signifiers which moor it" (11). Surveying the concept's formulations in Freud and deciding that they do not add up to a unitary theory of anxiety, in *The Language of Psychoanalysis* Laplanche and Pontalis split the difference with two separate entries on "Anxiety Neurosis" and "Anxiety Hysteria" (J. Laplanche and J.B. Pontalis, *The Language of Psychoanalysis*, trans. Donald Nicholson-Smith [New York: W. W. Norton, 1973], 37-40). The most extended account of anxiety seems to occur in the analysis of the phobia of Little Hans.

39. Ngai, *Ugly Feelings*, 210.

40. Ngai, *Ugly Feelings*, 7.

41. Carey, "A Work in Praise of Terrorism?," 16.

42. As Kerrigan, Rumrich, Fallon and others have noted, the argument that we are meant to critique rather than celebrate Samson's "great act" was first made in 1986 by Joseph Wittreich in *Interpreting Samson Agonistes* (Milton, *The Complete Poetry and Essential Prose*, 703). Carey added polemical urgency to a critical position that does not, in and of itself, stand or fall based on his additional claims about the resemblance between the biblical source and contemporary politics. Debates about whether or not such a historical effect of resemblance produces a transformation of the meaning of a literary work can neither support nor undermine the specific argument about Milton's representation of Samson. The heat of the rhetorical moment in which Carey's essay appeared seems to have produced as an unfortunate side effect the impression that the success or failure of this reading could somehow index, and prove or disprove, a larger claim about the historical nature of an artwork's meaning.

43. Even Julia Lupton, in the context of an entirely separate set of theoretical commitments and concerns, seems to arrive at a distinctly Fish-ian suspension on this topic, when she writes at the end of her discussion of Samson's violence as an example of the Benjaminian category of "divine violence," that "Milton neither glorifies nor condemns such violence, but rather explores its conditions and calls us to judge it." ("Samson Dagonistes," 184). By stopping

short of a decision and leaving her readers precariously exposed to these contradictory outcomes, Lupton's very avoidance of the obvious options (glorify? condemn?) constitutes itself a kind of choice, and one that places her alongside the Fish position, albeit on her own terms.

44. Fish, *How Milton Works*, 252.

45. Fish, *How Milton Works*, 252, italics mine.

46. Participants in the *Samson Agonistes* "debate" (if that is what it is/was) are not arguing coherently from shared terms, but collaboratively dismantling the platform upon which such a debate might take place by insisting upon mutually incongruous semantic constructions of "terrorism," with Carey's decision to elastically apply a modern political term to a Renaissance poem from a Biblical source cue-ing a nominalist restriction of the phrase on the part of Fish. Thus, at a certain level the debate about whether or not one can talk intelligibly about early modern terrorists replicates the debate about whether or not one can talk intelligibly about early modern homosexuals. The historically correct cop-out simply avoids unpleasantness by circumscribing the conceptual availability of a threatening and "modern" phenomenon to Renaissance subjects and the problem is solved.

To ask the vulgar question: Would John Milton have thought of himself as endorsing something that he would have understood as equivalent to "terrorism" as this term is used today? Obviously, to ask the question at all is already to assume that terrorism is a unity about which a "we" has coalesced in a shared sense of what does and does not count as an act of terrorism, and consigns offstage the attendant debates about the difference between political liberation movements and terrorism and where to place acts of sabotage intended to disrupt the domination of a foreign power along the continuum of strategic acceptability. Would John Milton have approved of violent acts if they were committed on behalf of a religious position with which he sided? If we are to draw upon *Christian Doctrine* for evidence, the immediate answer is an obvious and resounding negative. People should be free to write about the Bible and express varying opinions upon it, and "Without this freedom to which I refer, there is no religion and no gospel. Violence alone prevails; and *it is disgraceful and disgusting that the Christian religion should be supported by violence*" (1143, italics mine). Yet if we rephrase the question in another way, a different response is generated. If God tells us to do something, ought we to do it? The answer to this sort of question, as Fish has delighted in reminding inattentive readers of Milton, is resoundingly yes.

47. For a reading of the place of melancholy in this interior/exterior architecture which both draws upon but diverges from these remarks, see Drew Daniel "My Self, My Selpucher: Assembling Melancholy Masculinity in *Samson Agonistes*," *The Melancholy Assemblage: Affect and Epistemology in the English Renaissance* (New York: Fordham University Press, 2013), 251-290.

48. Lupton, "Samson Agonistes," 202.

49. As one example among many, consider a *Washington Post* article that followed closely upon the announcement in 2003 from Shanghai Secondary Medical University that hybrid human/animal embryos had been bred and allowed to live for several days while stem cell tissue was being harvested: "In Minnesota, pigs are being born with human blood in their veins. In Nevada, there are sheep whose livers and hearts are largely human. In California, mice peer from their cages with human brain cells firing in their skulls. [. . .] Biologists call these hybrid animals chimeras, after the mythical Greek creature with a lion's head, a goat's body and a serpent's tail." Rick Weiss, "Of Mice, Men and In-Between: Scientists Debate Blending of Human, Animal Forms," *Washington Post*. November 20, 2004.

50. Foucault, "Nietzsche, Genealogy, History," 154.

51. Foucault, "Nietzsche, Genealogy, History," 144.

An Apology for Queering Milton

Response by VICTORIA SILVER

That Milton is not Shakespeare has been a common judgment, and one rarely decided in Milton's favor. So it should come as no surprise that, as Will Stockton observes, queer readers have voted with their feet for the capacious, inclusive universe of Shakespeare studies and its many possible worlds. But if Dr. Johnson (who also disliked Shakespeare's tragedies) was not entirely wrong to say that no one ever wished *Paradise Lost* longer, that is because Milton's epic tends to be viewed not as literature but as versified ontology—the work of someone who knew, or thought he knew, the fundamental order of things. Whether this is what Milton meant by having his speaker propose to "assert eternal providence and justify the ways of God to men," such assumptions are nothing new (Dr. Johnson himself having entertained them). Indeed, they appear congenital to the public reception, if not the poetic project of *Paradise Lost*. Homer and Virgil wrote epics filled with gods, but theology then is mythology to us now, and we do not take the judgments of Zeus or Jupiter personally. Dante, it is true, did undertake to picture metaphysical reality in the *Commedia*, with the result that popular demand for the *Inferno* vastly outstrips the *Purgatorio* and *Paradiso* because the penalties of sin are so much more entertaining than the rewards of saintliness. Indeed, the American reading public may adore the occult (zombies, vampires, demons), the supernatural (angels and the divine in mufti), and the extraterrestrial (alien abductions, Area 51); it may devour each new report back from heaven, the Light or the inside of the mothership; but it dislikes being judged, least of all eternally, by anyone not *simpatico*. In literary studies too and for much the same cause, the Judeo-Christian God still gets under our skin, which is why critics prefer their divinity, if they must have one at all, served up in multiple, obscure and exotic mediations, or dispensed with altogether, usually by calling it something else, like heteronormativity.

Early modern culture had a greater tolerance for this God than we do. Nonetheless, like ourselves, it was inclined to make deity over in its own image—an image almost as patriarchal as ever Jehovah had been and, as Milton often complains, altogether unlike the Jesus of the gospels. In making religious or civil law, the tendency was to ignore all but a few sentences of the New Testament, while borrowing liberally from the Old and whatever tribal tradition or immemorial custom lay to hand. Further, as Ian Maclean has argued, both ancient and scholastic authorities ensured that the culture clung to a set of gender values as venerable and largely identical with the Pythagorean contraries or "principles of things" that Aristotle discusses in the *Metaphysics*: "limit and unlimited, odd and even, one and plurality, right and left, male and female, rest and movement, straight and curved, light and darkness, good and evil, square and oblong" (986a-

Response: An Apology for Queering Milton

b). And precisely because it was a patriarchy in every sense, early modern culture conceived a horror of gender contingency, in the unsurprising belief that such instability threatened the very foundations of its order. So, in Ben Jonson's neat phrase from *Epicoene*, "female vice should be a virtue male, / Or masculine vice, a female virtue be" (12-13)—a gender dictum pervading the literature of the age but not always in the same way, or even with the dominant significance of world subversion, as Shakespeare's romantic comedies abundantly imply (Jonson 292).

Compared to Shakespeare (or Sidney or Spenser, Ariosto or Tasso), Milton's poetry would appear to suffer from grave disadvantages in this regard, not all of which are owing to the Father's presence on the set: because everyone is naked, there are no pants roles in *Paradise Lost* (although Eve does wear them in Book Nine while Dalila hid them beneath her skirts*)*. Nor does epic afford the theatrical occasion for boys to play girls (although Raphael and the Lord seem to think Adam comes close, and Samson fears the same for himself). Of course, Milton's only play is a closet drama (the theaters being closed for the Interregnum), and to that extent cannot be said to court the psychological plague of spontaneous deviance predicted by anti- theatricalists (although Drew Daniel suggests the tragic hero himself is one of them). Besides, Samson, once shorn and now eyeless in Gaza, has biblical authority for his emasculation, as Dalila does for her virility. In both of Milton's epics, the tropological contagion of effeminacy appears confined to the dim, sybaritic Belial (Daniel), but only if we ignore the classical and humanist *topos* of tyranny that decks out Milton's devil, whose operatic loquacity, histrionic duplicity, vulgar opulence and sheer snobbery clearly announce the return of the repressed king, or queen. It also signals Satan's capacity for the polymorphous-perverse pleasure-seeking that republican polemic ascribed to tyrants and court parasites, and that Lynn Hunt has termed the "pornography" of political absolutism. Similarly, when prelates and priests make their figurative appearance, which they do promiscuously in the tracts and when one least expects it in the poetry, the imagery of autoeroticism expands exponentially. And that is because, if one is a dissenting Protestant in this tragic age of religious civil war, Roman and Anglican Catholicism are made the font of all perceived perversions.

Yet the ribald sexual imagination and robust bawdy which permeate most early modern literature and of course Shakespeare seem barely to break the surface of Milton's poetry, although when they do (Daniel), they can unmold the apparent sense of an entire passage. At the same time, his writing does not lack for full-fledged eroticism. Adam, Satan and especially the epic narrator all have a thing for our General Mother, and so do Eden's fruits and flowers. Eve herself moons over her fair outside, that is, until her reverie is broken by the divine imperative of species reproduction; but at the first sight of Adam's sexual difference, she turns to flee back to her own delectable likeness. Yet even before *Paradise Lost*, the Circean sorcerer and proxy courtier, Comus, who is all urgent sentience and libertine sexuality, cannot keep his febrile touch off that notable invert, Milton's Lady or the Lady Milton, whom he would divert, pervert and convert to his own circaddian rhythms (Melissa Sanchez). Owing to their refined substance, angelic bodies achieve a degree of interpenetration about which Donne's or Rochester's speakers can only fantasize, making Raphael blush at the very thought, and not out of shame (since the unfallen are guiltless) but pleasure (Stephen Guy-Bray). And for those still curious, it appears true from the catalogue of demons that the capacity of angels to assume both male and female shapes does extend the sexual range of the apostate (Guy-Bray and Daniel).

As the form of divine good, the power of beauty to entrance its beholders crosses not only genders but species and aeons (Guy-Bray). However perfect in his kind, Adam is entirely smitten by Raphael's "glorious shape" (Guy-Bray) "whose excellence he saw / Transcend his own so far" that he doubts his own merely human adequacy (*PL* 5.456-58). Similarly, a pompous Satan, whose "glory obscured" moves all hell and Milton's speaker (*PL* 1.594), pines for his lost beauty reflected in the unfallen cherubim he had thought to disdain, chagrined "chiefly to find here observed / His lustre visibly impaired" (*LM:PL* 4.844-50). For much the same reason as Eve's absorption in her own watery image, the apostate hordes cannot avert their gaze from their great chief, which has truly spectacular consequences for all concerned in Book Ten. But while heroic homosociality seems to rule in Milton's hell, with all that this might portend of subterranean passions, the apostate angels appear incapable of doing anything about it, so absorbed is each one in his own pathos. Narcissism also abounds in the nostalgia of the fallen for a lost heaven, where it complicates Satan's feelings for his erstwhile God, whether Father, Son and Messiah, or Our Saviour in *Paradise Regained*, for whom he adopts the debonaire guise of "one in city, or court, or palace bred" (*LM:PR* 2.300), and lays a "table spread, in regal mode" with "Tall stripling youths rich-clad, of fairer hue/ Than Ganymede or Hylas," along with nymphs, Naiades and "ladies of the Hesperides" (*LM:PR* 2.340, 352-57).

Admittedly, these are themes and motifs whose significance finally depends on the poet's usage; but Will is nonetheless right to say there is a case for queering Milton, unless one takes the carefully bald "argument" that prefaces each book of *Paradise Lost* as the totality of Milton's poetic intent or the poem's meaning. If we did, then there would be no Milton studies, and very likely no readers of Milton either. As always, the problem here is interpretive orthodoxy, which fluctuates with every new generation and every new trend; indeed, orthodoxies are conceived and promulgated for that very reason—opinion shifts, and it especially shifts when the question is a matter of interpretation (and what, said jesting Pilate, is not). Consensus is something different—a description of the state of our belief, not a proscription of it: consensus should still allow for dissent whereas dogma struggles to contain the instinctive human drive to make satisfactory sense of experience—to find the world meaningful and profound as well as uncertain, trivial, difficult, perplexing, appalling and even unspeakable. One would think that literary critics would know better by now, given the conviction of other academic fields (philosophy in particular) that our analyses lack rigorousness, rest on wholly insufficient grounds, are merely "subjective," whatever that means.

But the hope for some self-skepticism as well as critical tolerance of others' opinions must confront our visceral attachment to our own ideas as true, right and just—God to us—whether they can take the form of received assumptions or the intellectual intuitions that we struggle in our work to make articulate and evident. Such passionate belief, or more properly, identification with what we ourselves think makes every student of any subject dismissive in private, where we can be pleasurably alone with our own dogmas. But since we publish those opinions as part of our profession, literary critics like all academics must confront the fact of a plurality of views, however configured by intellectual vogues or disciplinary consensus. And while we may silently crave to make our dogma everyone else's, it never can and never should be, because to do so transforms truth-seeking into power-mongering. Worse still, like the apostate angels who are self-condemned to repetition of the same, we will never learn a new thing.

Orthodoxy was of course a problem for Milton too, and those critics who take Milton as their subject would always do well to consult the author on the question of intellectual inquiry. In 1667, when *Paradise Lost* was first published, Milton was mostly known as a Cromwellian *apparachik*, an apologist for regicide as well as the crass debunker of "the king's book," *Eikon Basilike*; moreover, rumor apparently had it that he was a bigamist. Such notoriety was sufficient at the Restoration to secure his (temporary) arrest and to raise questions about the decision not to except him from the Act of Indemnity and Oblivion. From what we can tell, Milton was eccentric even from his Cambridge days, when he refused ordination in favor of a self-ordained plan of study whose fruits never cease to amaze. Later of course, he became a full-blown rebel against church and state, and from time to time, an outlaw, depending on whom was in charge. This fact has figured in Milton studies by his being Satanized in the Romantic fashion, which because Milton is himself a god of the English literary canon, has always lent that critical turn to the Dark Side a certain *frisson*, as it does the not-dissimilar activity of figuring out new ways to deflate his huge poetic afflatus.

But in his lifetime, being John Milton did not mean being on top. As a controversialist in the early 1640s, Milton was without much authority—too young, too obscure, too left field. Nonetheless, his tracts managed to scandalize one party or another: first, the bishops and their supporters, then parliament and the Presbyterians, after that monarchists both national and international, not to mention public sentiment on the eve of monarchy's and Anglicanism's restoration, and in 1673 with his last tract, Gilbert Sheldon's resettled church, the Cavalier parliament and no doubt the king too—that is, in the unlikely event that it was read by any of them. But once *Paradise Lost* was discovered by the Duke of Dorset, browsing among the booksellers' stalls in Little Britain as legend has it, the poem's sudden emergence was greeted as if it were the birth of Athena from the head of Zeus, at least by the *cognoscenti* of the new regime. The rapt enthusiasm with which Dryden celebrates Milton's achievement is indicative:

> Three poets, in three distant ages born,
> Greece, Italy, and England did adorn.
> The first in loftiness of thought surpass'd,
> The next in majesty, in both the last:
> The force of Nature could no farther go;
> To make a third, she join'd the former two. (Patterson *liii*)

Queer Milton

If no Byronic frenzy greeted his new eminence, Milton's audacity in picturing (as they saw it) the one true God did shock some, who considered the poem blasphemous on that count and others, inasmuch as *Paradise Lost* was figuratively populated with all the poet's Christian heresies, including the most heinous at that or any other time, antitrinitarianism (*Christian Doctrine*, his theological treatise, no doubt went unpublished because the 1662 Act of Uniformity criminalized Socinianism, the catch-word for that heresy). But his fellow scribblers saw to it that Milton's sudden eminence was perpetuated—Addison especially, who made himself the impresario of Miltoniana—until Milton's literary stature and his own Tory politics compelled Dr. Johnson to put poet and poem in their proper place, this time as a palinode in which Sin erupts out of Milton's republican egotism. The rest, as they say, is history, with the battle well joined between lovers and haters of the poet, with some of both persuasions in Milton studies. At a conference some years ago, where I delivered a paper on defamation in Milton's anti-prelatical tracts, I had the peculiar felicity of a distinguished scholar pronouncing at its end that my subject was a regicide, a murderer and a libeller, whom he implied nothing could redeem. But one doesn't have to be royalist and Anglican, or a Restoration scholar, to detest the poet: as I said, recent generations of Miltonists, brought up on the hermeneutics of suspicion, have made it a critical sport to catch their subject out in his neuroses, logical contradictions and ideological lapses—like Dr. Johnson, exposing the idol's feet of clay.

But then, which of us is perfect? I am myself no stranger to controversy in Milton studies, which is one reason why Will solicited my response to the fine essays assembled for this issue of *Early Modern Culture* on "queering Milton." Indeed, a couple of students informed me (I am not currently working in the field) that a Miltonist of note evidently found my own reading of the subject so objectionable that he declared in a footnote that he would not deign to consider it. Since being thus excepted could pique the reader's interest, I should thank him, as he should thank me for moving him to set the record straight as he sees it. However, Will's trepidation in the face of the Milton establishment, which to my certain knowledge is far from monolithic, does give me pause, along with student reports from the front, by which I mean the Milton list-serv whose bouts of incivility place it right up there with World of Warcraft as a model of intellectual engagement. But while there are certainly a few in the field who relish what Milton euphemistically called "the wars of Truth," bad manners and closed minds are hardly unique to Milton studies; and in the poet's own day, intellectual controversy could reach heights of abuse for the most part undreamed of in our academy. And it must be confessed that the aggressiveness that obtains and is even celebrated in some academic quarters can derive from a sense of the urgency and importance of the questions in hand, no doubt aggravated by the perpetual gap between human aspiration and human means (or what's a heaven for?).

Whether adequately or not, Milton defended his own infamously "tart rhetoric" on such grounds, seeing himself engaged in matters which, while irreducibly interpretive, were nonetheless of the greatest moment. But except when the English major is made a national laughingstock, as it currently is by politicians, the media and the rest of campus, the larger world remains perfectly indifferent to literary criticism, whose activity and purposes it neither understands nor values. From such a vantage, our wars cannot but appear petty and ourselves ridiculous. At the same time, we must not acquiesce in our trivialization: Milton did not, whose artistic stature was always impending until his final decade, and whose personal (as against Cromwellian) tracts do not seem to have risen above the generality of the pamphlet wars, with the negative exception of *The Doctrine and Discipline of Divorce* (1644). But soon enough, they were recalled and read at other "revolutions"—in 1689, 1776 and 1789—and not only by Whigs and Romantics. They are now anthologized along with those of key republicans and dissenters, and even noticed by some political historians.

And yet Milton and his controversial writings were judged ridiculous, even unconscionable, and as he himself pointed out, usually by those whose received authority or incumbency led them to suppose that God fought for them. But despite an egotism infinitely more justifiable than his opponents' or indeed any Milton critic's, and his sometimes indecorous zeal on behalf of the Good Old Cause, I sincerely doubt Milton believed God spoke to him in the night watches, or in any other than the usual way—through scripture—although it was regularly inferred from occasional passages in the tracts and of course the proems of *Paradise Lost* that he did. Owing to their religious and presumptively metaphysical nature, as I mentioned, his poetic expressions have been assigned a peculiar literality by some readers; but this inclination to literalism is also the fault of his own penchant for autobiographical excursus in the tracts—a defense against the *ad hominem* polemics of the day, or put another way, an abiding hunger to be recognized in his own terms. Because that recognition did not come until he probably knew its dubious value, Milton saw the human experience of deity and truth as interpretive, moral and historical, which is to say, conditional upon the evidence of scriptural expression, the integrity of each person's understanding and choice, and the flux of circumstance with which he believed divine providence surrounds us for a purpose.

I have argued that this is the invariable predicament of human faith in an insuperably hidden God, to which the Hebrew and Christian scriptures as well as the Protestant reformers return again and again, not to mention the Miltonic "I" who must regularly make that recognition in one form or another, and to which it must accommodate its all-too-human desires as Milton found himself obliged to do, both early and late. It is also the ordinary predicament of human knowledge, where we believe much and (in the philosophical sense) know little. Milton is no biblicist: he acknowledges the corrupt transmission of scripture (the Christian texts especially), and the difficulties posed by scriptural locutions more generally—the "hard places" on which he declines to build, focusing instead on what is clearly if not always positively expressed. As early as the Prolusions, he conspicuously adopted a Baconian skepticism about the untrammelled workings of the human mind (usually of the scholastic and metaphysical persuasion): indeed, Bacon's idols and Milton's idolatry share this same deluded source, which in its operations tends to mistake the specious for the real, the received and familiar for the right and true, and to conceive justice as the demand that everyone think and act as "I" do.

But he also combined such skepticism with Bacon's exuberant sense of human possibility—that is, once such idolatrous tendencies were recognized and contained by an apt and conscientious *organon* or method of inquiry.

As I see it, method for Milton meant the adoption and observance of what amounts to an imminent, rhetorically-sensitive hermeneutic—the "grammatical-historical" method of exegesis, which was not original to him but to the rise of early modern humanism. Its northern cynosure was Erasmus, from whom, ironically, Luther learned about the Hebrew genitive and thereby justification *sola gratia, sola fides, sola scriptura*, which in large measure begat the Protestant Reformation. As Milton himself describes them in *Christian Doctrine*, the exegetical criteria for valid inference are

> linguistic ability, knowledge of the original sources, consideration of the overall intent, distinction between literal and figurative language, examination of the causes and circumstances, and of what comes before and after the passage in question, and comparison of one text with another. It must always be asked, too, how far the interpretation is in agreement with faith. Finally, one often has to take into account the anomalies of syntax, as, for example, when a relative does not refer to its immediate antecedent but to the principle word in the sentences, although it is not so near it. . . . Lastly, no inferences should be made from the text, unless they follow necessarily from what is written. This precaution is necessary, otherwise we may be forced to believe something which is not written instead of something which is, and to accept human reasoning, generally fallacious, instead of divine doctrine, thus mistaking the shadow for the substance. What we are obliged to believe are the things written in the sacred books, not the things debated in academic gatherings. (*YP* 6:582-83)

In short, Miltonic exegesis conceived the divine word not as transcendent but as incarnate, embedded like human beings themselves in the maze of lived as against speculative circumstance, right down to the operations of syntax. As he argues in *The Doctrine and Discipline of Divorce*, exegesis is itself equitable speech that resolves the anomalous or exceptional expression by attending to the context of utterance—"what comes before and after the passage in question": for "there is scarce any one saying in the Gospel, but must be read with limitations and distinctions, to be rightly understood . . . .which requires a skilfull and laborious gatherer [to] compare the words he finds, with other precepts, with the end of every ordinance, and with the general *analogy* of Evangelick doctrine." "Otherwise," Milton observes, "many particular sayings would be but strange repugnant riddles." (*YP* 2:338)

Response: An Apology for Queering Milton

Thus Milton resists both a crude and a metaphysical literalism, the first confining scriptural expression to its merely ostensible or superficial sense, the second converting figurative speech into symbols of supernatural entities (the source of Trinitarianism in Milton's view). In either case, a failure to consider variations in usage denies the fact that neither speech nor its speakers can escape the human condition, whose intelligibility is embodied in particular experiences, occasions, desires and needs. Yet if exegesis should not stray from the natural or grammatical force of scriptural expressions—should not concoct or impose a semantic order for its books that lacks an evidentiary basis—Milton's rhetorical emphasis on "the overall intent" recognizes the complex configuration of motives, "causes and circumstances," which inform anything we say or do. And he practiced this equitable method with considerable insight and such scrupulous care that while it was the singular source of his heterodoxy, his readings of the scriptural text still stand up. But because he admits the ordinary contingencies of existence, Milton has been accused of illogic and expedience, although at this late date we should know that the formalities of logic and the so-called "laws of thought" pertain to a specific disciplinary use of language that is performed in philosophy departments, and which (as Wittgenstein observed decades ago, Hobbes in the seventeenth century, and rhetoricians a couple of millenia earlier) bears little resemblance to how we actually use and make sense of words.

These charges are usually made where it is presumed that Milton has a personal ax to grind, with his invocation in that tract of "charity" and "equity" mistakenly made self-serving when these values are long-standing principles of interpretation in theology and law, both exegetical disciplines which argue against *strictum jus*—the obtuse expectation that the meaning of human speech and action is general and unconditioned, like logic itself proposes to be. Although scripture in Milton's view has a single sense, the gospel or *kerygma* announcing Jesus as the Christ, he was not so zany as to suppose that recourse to method would somehow produce in every mind an identical reading, much less a univocal doctrine in all matters; nor was that a desideratum of his faith. Reasonable inference, well-grounded in the text, was desirable, while coercion in pursuit of even outward uniformity—the policy of every regime under which he lived (however moderated under the Protectorate)—was anathema to him. If forcible conformity in religion preceded the reformation in England, it also ensued from it—the Henrician settlement having made church and state constitutionally one, thereby turning religious dissent into sedition and treason where before it had been heresy (the punishment was capital either way). Furthermore, especially under Elizabeth and James, conformity to the state church was popularly regarded as patriotic, which is why Milton's express tolerance for sectarianism in the tracts makes him, if not unique, then notable; and this was not only because he had become a sect unto himself.

For one thing, as a Protestant, he persisted despite many disappointments in thinking that humanity is educable; moreover, unlike the Erastian Luther or the theocratic Calvin, he felt that the principle of Christian liberty ought to have public as well as private consequences; and however mistakenly in the event, he put his political faith in the experience of freedom itself, on the model of the Protestant

Reformation. Moreover, he was also a member of the Cromwellian government, who by his own account chose to lose his remaining eyesight in order to write his first *Defense of the English People*, which hardly suggests the transcendental turn or antinomian paralysis ascribed to him. Nor is the appropriate comparison here with democratic radicals like Lilburne, Overton and Walwyn, next to whom his liberalism may appear weak-kneed. It should be with the beliefs which commonly governed seventeenth-century politics, whether a Presbyterian commonwealth or the restored monarchy.

As any number of historians have pointed out, the greatest of these was "order," simply because its achievement was felt—accurately or not—to be the most important, the most fragile and, as represented by the rule of law, a less pervasive aspect of early modern English life. From this angle, Milton's constant extenuation over two decades for civil and religious tumult and change, including civil war, the overthrow of the English constitution, and the king's judicial execution, is truly audacious (and it would have been more dangerous if more people had read him). The conditions he regarded as necessary and inevitable to the vital work of reform looked to the majority of the nation like a world grown suddenly unrecognizable and repulsive—capricious, discordant, perverse, the world famously "turned upside down." But then, as Milton reminds us, what custom or orthodoxy inclines us to take for truth can lead to our outlawing the real thing; for "if it comes to prohibiting, there is not ought more likely to be prohibited than truth it self; whose first appearance to our eyes blear'd and dimm'd with prejudice and custom, is more unsightly and unplausible than many errors" (*YP* 2:565).

In that final tract to which I referred, *Of True Religion, Heresy, Schism, Toleration* (1673), he sought (culpably in our view) to exploit for Protestant dissenters the tactical advantage offered by a national outburst of "anti-popery," consequent upon Charles' Declaration of Indulgence (1672), which had just been rescinded by the king in the face of implacable opposition from the Cavalier parliament. Ostensibly, the Indulgence sought to ease the lot of all nonconformists which had been rendered still more painful and abject by the second Conventicles Act of 1670, whose new severity Marvell memorably termed "the quintessence of arbitrary malice." Moreover, Charles was about to embark on a second war with the Dutch, and his ministers (the infamous Cabal) thought by the Indulgence to pacify the homefront, murmuring under an increasingly heavy tax burden. But unfortunately, the Dutch were Protestants with an exceedingly active printing industry (of which both English intellectual and religious dissenters had long availed themselves), while the government had allied itself with Catholic France, a fact with which the Dutch made great play in their propaganda. Given the general virulence of English "anti-popery" and a growing distrust of their king among the voting classes, the Declaration was popularly taken as an attempt by a crypto-Catholic to rescue the legal position of his co-religionists. But Charles' government would also seem to have had a larger legal aim, as parliament contended in its replies to the king; and that was to assert in the best Stuart fashion the royal prerogative, in effect testing the suspending and dispensing powers which arguably attended the monarch's position as supreme governor of the state church. It was a move that could be and was seen as a possible first step towards reestablishing Roman Catholicism in England (in exchange for subsidy, Charles had just promised Louis as much in the Secret Treaty of Dover of 1670, although evidently without any immediate intention of fulfilling his commitment).

Since Milton shared the patriotic English aversion to "popery," he rejected the proffered Indulgence owing to its arguably unconstitutional means (Bunyan would do the same with James' less problematical Declarations in 1687 and 1688, which William Penn for his part would embrace, earning odium for himself in most of the dissenting community). However, as Keith Stavely argues, Milton evidently hoped the "no popery" agitation would result in a compensatory bill, then under discussion in committee, limiting the penal measures against dissenters in the name of Protestant unity. To promote that bill, which eventually died with the session in the House of Lords, he wrote this patently polemical tract, *True Religion*, but to no avail because Charles, faced with signs of what would become Exclusionist sentiment, prorogued parliament. However, the session did produce the first Test Act banning Catholics from political office of any kind, whose oath of allegiance, now denying the Tridentine dogma of transubstantiation, exposed by default the Catholicism of the Duke of York, Lord Admiral, and Charles' treasurer, Lord Clifford, who privately resigned their offices—if not their integrity.

Between his animadversions on "the common adversary" (*YP* 8:420), "the Papal Anti-christian Church" and what he regards as its habitual idolatry (*YP* 8:434), Milton surveys the doctrines of the various Protestant denominations— "Lutherans, Calvinists, Anabaptists, Socinians, Arminians" but tellingly not Quakers—having declared at the outset against "the Papist" that "All these may have some errors, but are no hereticks" (*YP* 8:423). It is a distinction frequently observed by those writers and politicians who promoted liberty of conscience for all, and, as Blair Worden has argued, constituted government policy under the Protectorate, which the Calendar of State Papers Domestic shows in action. But in a strictly legal sense, he can say this because heresy was no longer a crime in England—Elizabeth's Act of Uniformity (1559) having once again repealed the medieval statutes revived by Mary Tudor. Moreover, in 1677, perhaps out of the mixed motives which gave Milton his brief hope, the same parliament that devised the Clarendon Code and issued the Test Act would abolish the last relic of heresy legislation—the writ *de heretico comburendo*, unused since 1612 when it was issued to burn two Anabaptists under the personal supervision of James I (Browning 8:400). So Milton can fairly claim that "Popery is the only or the greatest Heresie" extant in Christendom, "and he who is so forward to brand all others for Hereticks, the obstinate Papist, the only Heretick" (*YP* 8:421), insofar as the papacy demanded the complete, unreflective submission of faith to "a Religion taken up and believe'd from the traditions of men and additions to the word of God" (*YP* 8:421), which is heresy in Milton's definition.

What *True Religion* scathingly calls "the growth of this Romish weed" had in the past usually exercised Milton's pen only when he lambasted Anglican or Presbyterian churches for perpetuating the relics of "popish" practices (prelacy, liturgy, canon law), or for emulating the papacy's repressive policies (uniformity and censorship) (*YP* 8:417). But here he does not (only) tar both with a popish brush, but draws the Reformers' fundamental distinction on behalf of toleration: Roman Catholicism "permits not her Laity to read the Bible in their own tongue" (*YP* 8:434) and, by a range of further interdictions, prohibits the active inquiry made possible at least in theory when the Henrician settlement placed the Great Bible in every parish (it should be noted that the medieval heresy statutes and one of Henry's own were still in force at the time, since Henry himself purposed no change in the English church from Catholic doctrine or worship). By contrast, Milton defines Protestants as those who recognize two fundamental principles, namely, "that the Rule of true Religion is the Word of God only; and that their Faith ought not to be an implicit faith" (*YP* 8:420), that is, it should be understood as well as believed:

> Heresie is in the Will and choice profestly against Scripture; error is against the Will, in misunderstanding the Scripture after all sincere endeavours to understand it rightly: Hence it was said well by one of the Ancients, *Err I may, but a Heretick I will not be*. It is a humane frailty to err, and no man is infallible here on earth. But so long as all these profess to set the Word of God only before them as the Rule of faith and obedience; and use all diligence and sincerity of heart, by reading, by learning, by study, by prayer for Illumination of the Holy Spirit, to understand the Rule and obey it, they have done what man can do: God will assuredly pardon them, as he did the friends of *Job*; good and pious men, though much mistaken, as there it appears, in some points of doctrine. (*YP* 8:423-24)

Milton's point here—and my own as a literary critic—is that there is no heresy wherever an effort is made to understand and elucidate the text which, God "having made no man infallible" (including the pope), is "what man can do" (*YP* 8:424). Interpretation is a matter of probabilities, not certainties. Thus to exact from others unwavering adherence to received opinion, usually in *adiaphora* or "things indifferent" and therefore inessential to salvation, is a far greater abuse of faith than permitting disagreement over what should in fact be left elective, free of merely human impositions in the form of "a command or a Prohibition, and so consequently an addition to the word of God" (*YP* 8:428). "Besides," Milton observes, "how unequal, how uncharitable must it needs be, to Impose that which his conscience cannot urge him to impose, upon him whose conscience forbids him to obey?" (*YP* 8:428). In a fugue of *erotema*, Milton pursues this problem of arbitrary and self-aggrandizing authority in matters where no certainty can be had, demanding of the reader: "If he who thinks himself in the truth professes to have learnt it, not by implicit faith, but by attentive study of the Scriptures & full perswasion of heart, with what equity can he refuse to hear or read him, who demonstrates to have gained his knowledge by the same way? Is it a fair course to assert truth by arrogating to himself the only freedome of speech, and stoping the mouths of others equally gifted?" (*YP* 8:436).

Equity or fairness means charitable allowance and equal right to an unburdened conscience and to opinions freely expressed—in a word, toleration, which Milton was brave to use. For "What Protestant then who himself maintains the same Principles, and disavowes all implicit Faith, would persecute, and not rather charitably tolerate such men as these, unless he mean to abjure the Principles of his own Religion?" (*YP* 8:426). *Erotema* are conspicuous in *True Religion* and not just because Milton feels the urgency of the moment and the issue he has in hand. He intends with each rhetorical question to pose home truths, to interrogate the reader's conscience—to challenge us to admit the inferences he successively draws from the tract's definition of heresy and what are taken to be Protestant first principles by the various denominations who subscribe to that title. The originally geometrical maxim he invokes (and calls logical)—"*against them who deny Principles, we are not to dispute*" (*YP* 8:432)—pertains to more than the futility of arguing with those who do not share our assumptions, namely, Roman Catholics who refuse to acknowledge scripture as the sole and proper source of Christian knowledge. Its invocation here signals what Milton's polemic may disguise, that the argument for toleration in *True Religion* should have the force of deductive necessity for anyone who claims to be a Protestant.

The problem, as he knew from experience, is that both Anglicans and Presbyterians, while professing to accept these Protestant principles, pervert them by admitting political imperatives extraneous to ecclesiastical concerns. However intelligible given the early modern concern for "order," or legally justifiable given the constitutional identity of church and state in English law, uniformity of religious observance is just such a political perversion (paradoxically justified by the claim that what was "inessential" or "indifferent" left government free to legislate in that arena). But it is cruel and inhumane nonsense—Marvell's "arbitrary malice"—when considered from the vantage of faith in what Luther calls *res non apparentes*, things which do not appear as such. Milton goes on to define the extent of this toleration and the exercise of Christian liberty by English subjects, "as being all Protestants, that is on all occasions to give account of their Faith, either by Arguing, Preaching in their several Assemblies, Publick writing, and the freedom of Printing" (*YP* 8:426).

Invoking Paul in Thessalonians, he asks "How shall we prove all things, which includes all opinions at least founded on Scripture, unless we not only tolerate them, but patiently hear them, and seriously read them?" (*YP* 8:436). What Stavely mistakenly regards as an originally Latitudinarian distinction between involuntary error and willful heresy Milton had argued since the 1640s and *The Reason of Church Government* (1642), where he represents the rise of Protestant sectarianism in England as a necessary, refining contest between truth and error, an *agon* which the nation, like Samson, should undergo if it would be open to the reforming hand of divine providence. To this extent, the tracts consistently propound a restrictive antinomianism that seeks to remove whatever obstacles—episcopacy, canon law, presbytery, censorship, monarchy, the constitutional union of church and state—whose effect is to constrain Christian liberty and stand in the way of God's revelation to the English people, "being all Protestants."

This last stipulation, and his strictures against Roman Catholic worship and devotion as "idolatrous," can be taken as a show of bigotry, or at least a demagogic blot on Milton's liberal scutcheon. However, we do well to remember that the charge of heresy was first levelled by the papacy, which excommunicated Henry and then Edward, rested with Mary's brief spell of *auto de fe*, and then paused in order to take the measure of Elizabeth's regime. Having done so to his satisfaction Pius V issued the Bull *Regnans in excelsis* in 1570, denouncing Elizabeth as "a heretic and favourer of heretics," excommunicating her and absolving her subjects of their obedience, so as to prepare the way for the queen's ultimate assassination (Elton 427). When combined with Mary Stuart's arrival incontinent from Scotland in 1568, as Catholic Europe's great white hope; the immense pressure exerted by the Jesuit missionary movement, begun in 1577; the chronic arrival on British shores of the Spanish Armada from 1588 on, and Spain's war with the Protestant Netherlands, the English public came to regard Roman Catholicism not as a Christian faith or even a church but as "popery" and a hostile polity. And then there was "Treason's Masterpeece," the Gunpowder Plot of 1605 to assassinate James and parliament together, devised by a handful of English Catholics whose overthrow inspired the Observance of the Fifth of November or "Thanksgiving" Act in 1606, with its fireworks, bonfires and burning of popes in effigy.

Owing to what he describes as the papacy's habit of international aggression but more particularly its internal policy of violence against dissent, Milton shares that prejudice but on the principle that "Ecclesiastical is ever pretended to Political"—a pretension as Anglican as it was papal, although he is careful not to say so here (*YP* 8:429):

> The Pope by this mixt faculty, pretends right to Kingdoms and States, and especially to this of *England*, Thrones and Unthrones Kings, and absolves the people from their obedience to them; sometimes interdicts to whole Nations the Publick worship of God, shutting up their Churches: and was wont to dreign away greatest part of the wealth of this then miserable Land, as part of his Patrimony, to maintain the Pride and Luxury of his Court and Prelates, and now since, through the infinite mercy and favour of God, we have shaken off his *Babylonish* Yoke, hath not ceas'd by his Spyes and Agents, Bulls and Emissaries, once to destroy both King and Parliament; perpetually to seduce, corrupt, and pervert as many as they can of the People. Whether therefore it be fit or reasonable, to tolerate men thus principl'd in Religion towards the State, I submit it to the consideration of all Magistrates, who are best able to provide for their own and the publick safety. (*YP* 8:430)

Response: An Apology for Queering Milton

With this final gesture at the Cavalier parliament—itself the implacable foe of English dissent—Milton makes clear that the true idol of Roman Catholicism is the pope and his claim of infallibility, to which *A Treatise of Civil Power* (1659) amply attests in its argument for the separation of church and state, ecclesiastical from political jurisdictions. It is on the grounds of such idolatry that he affirms the English response to the papal bull damning Elizabeth—the 1571 Act (13 Elizabeth I c.2) "against the bringing in and putting in execution of bulls and other instruments from the see of Rome" (Elton 428). The statute was intended not only to prohibit the publishing of *Regnan in excelsis* in England, but also as a kind of symbolic equivalent to the Act of Supremacy's assertion of *praemunire*—the monarch's exclusive legal jurisdiction in his or her regality. It achieves this by prohibiting the importation of all religious paraphernalia carrying the pope's blessing and therewith his authority: "any token or tokens, thing or things, called by the name of an *Agnus Dei*, or any crosses, pictures, beads or suchlike vain and superstitious from the bishop or see of Rome, or from any person or persons authorised or claiming authority by or from the said bishop or see of Rome to consecrate or hallow the same" (Elton 431).

Like the rest of Elizabethan "anti-popery" legislation, the purpose of whose savagery was apparently deterrence since it was erratically enforced except against Jesuits and priests, this statute was still on the books a hundred years later, and for the same reasons which told against the Declaration of Indulgence in 1673 and again in 1688—fear that a Catholic king would reestablish that religion and papal jurisdiction in England. If the effect of the Tudor bill was to deprive Roman Catholics of any new articles of devotion and worship (and what they had were later subject to confiscation under the still more egregious 1593 Act for "securing the Queen's subjects in obedience" [35 Elizabeth 1 c.2]), it was only implemented during political panics like this one in 1673. Unfortunately, with the Declaration of Indulgence and the Test Act, which revealed in quick succession that James had not only converted to Rome but was about to wed Mary of Modena, a Catholic princess, the nation's combustible prejudices were fully ignited: "On 5 November [1673], there were more bonfires and more popes burnt in effigy than there had been for thirty years," John Miller reports (Miller 131).

No doubt during the Commonwealth, his nation had in Milton's view once more shaken off the Babylonian yoke of prelacy and the magistrate's coercive power in religion, only to have the Presbyterians reimpose it in another form, and the Protectorate remove it again, until the Restoration when it was yet once more reestablished. But for the same politic reasons that lead him to invoke the Thirty-Nine Articles and the prudence of magistracy, much goes unsaid in *True Religion*. The advice it gives for rooting out the "Romish weed" is all but straightforwardly advice for reforming religious policy: first, "to read duly and diligently the Holy Scriptures," since the neglect of such study leads to "implicit faith, ever learning and never taught, much hearing and small proficience, till want of Fundamental knowledg easily turns to superstition and Popery" (*YP* 8:433-34). Next, to extend a national policy of tolerance towards other Protestant sects, including "freedome of speech," for "no Learned man but will confess he hath much profited by reading Controversies, his Senses awakt, his Judgement sharpen'd, and the truth he holds more firmly establish't" (*YP* 8:437). And finally, "to amend our lives," which notoriously in the reign of "the merry monarch" (an epithet always invoked by historians in this context) had "grown more numerously and excessively vitious than heretofore; Pride, Luxury, Drunkenness, Whoredom, Cursing, Swearing, bold and open Atheism every where abounding" (*YP* 8:438). There is also, as Stavely remarks, the unmistakable hint that God is already punishing England for its copious immorality by "Pestilence, Fire, Sword and Famin" (*YP* 8:439), in the shape of the great plague of 1665, the great fire of London in 1666, and the defeats suffered in Charles' first war against the Dutch, on the tremulous eve of that war's renewal.

Yet in the midst of the anti-popish hysteria which *True Religion* does nothing to abate, Milton nonetheless extends to Roman Catholics the same immunity from coercive civil measures for which he argues in the case of Protestants: "Are we to punish them by corporal punishment, or fines in their Estates, upon account of their Religion? I suppose it stands not with the Clemency of the Gospel, more then what appertains to the security of the State" (*YP* 8:431). In short, he rejects the core of Elizabethan recusancy legislation—the model for the Clarendon Code—which fined, on an escalating scale that became ever more insupportable, those recusants from Anglican worship who attended nonconformist services on Sundays, whether Protestant or Catholic, issuing writs of *praemunire* (which meant the loss of all property and indefinite imprisonment) against whomever openly displayed their religious dissent. Since he lived under a regime that, since the Interregnum's end, insisted in Halifax's famous phrase that "It is impossible that a Dissenter should not be a Rebel," historical precedent is not always Milton's friend. Yet if his syntactical show of reluctance ("I suppose") is as politic as his Anglican (or simply English) "our," few dissenting tracts at the time made the same concession since all were united against the common papistical foe.

In fact, neither his conventional charges of Catholic heresy and idolatry, nor his expedient placation of Anglicanism and the Cavalier parliament, express the heart of Milton's matter: both are tactics adopted for the occasion and his would-be audience, and to focus upon them is to miss the tract's central point, which is to be found in its most powerful figure—that of Jesus' seamless tunic, "woven from top to bottom," which moved the soldiers who had crucified him to cast lots for the whole garment, rather than tear it into four parts, "one for each soldier" (John 19:23). On the face of it, there are few better images of religious unity or at least *outward* uniformity than this analogy; but for Milton it is an odd choice. In *The Reason of Church Government*, he compares ecclesiastical "discipline" on earth and in heaven to the baroque image (shortly to be superseded) of planetary epicycles, in which each cosmic body executes intermediate circles within its larger orbit (*vide* Adam's inquiries of Raphael). Thus, he suggests, church discipline may orb "it self into a thousand vagancies of glory and delight, and with a kinde of eccentricall equation be as it were an invariable Planet of joy and felicity" (*YP* 1:752). Then there is *Areopagitica*'s "Temple of the Lord" which simply defies the delusion of inseparable uniformity in the church; for "when every stone is laid artfully together, it cannot be united into a continuity, it can but be contiguous in this world; neither can every peece of the building be of one form; nay rather the perfection consists in this, that out of many moderat varieties and brotherly dissimilitudes that are not vastly disproportional arises the goodly and the gracefull symmetry that commends the whole pile and structure" (YP 2:555).

As these instances predict, Milton takes the image of Jesus' seamless tunic, which had evidently been used to justify such religious conformity, and makes it his own: "It is written that the Coat of our Saviour was without seame: whence some would infer that there should be no division in the Church of Christ. Yet seams in the same cloath, neither hurt the garment, nor misbecome it; and not only seams, but Schisms will be while men are fallible. . . ." (YP 8:436) "Seames" belong to our finite and fallible condition, not the idealism of those unnamed polemicists who took the circumstance of Jesus' woven tunic and converted it willy-nilly into a symbol of lockstep religion, without regard for "limitations and distinctions." Milton chooses not to argue the exegetical point; instead, he rejects what he terms in *Areopagitica* the "irrational" demand for seamless continuity in any human artifact. In this world, seams "neither hurt the garment, nor misbecome it," anymore than contiguity or eccentricity necessarily compromise perfection or joy, which brings me back to the question of what it means to "queer" Milton.

The answer depends to some extent on whose Milton: more often than not, the poet and polemicist is known by the constructions we critics place on the texts which bear his name. In the last fifty years or so, this Milton has been some version of rationalist or irrationalist, or both at once. But his writings remain far richer than any of the categories we use to describe them: when I am teaching Milton, and I go back to any work and read it from end to end, I see things that I have forgotten or never saw in the first place; and they are things that do not admit of simple assimilation to "my" Milton—grist for my peculiar critical mill. They require me to stop and think again, always marveling at his art, always astonished at its methodical detail. It is this sense of Milton's method, I assume, that led Stanley Fish to entitle his book, "How Milton Works," which he has gleefully described as thirty pages of telling and six hundred of showing. But does such an analytical mechanism, whose popularity remains undiminished after all these years, do complete justice to the possibilities of meaning in Milton's texts, or to the range of our possible engagements with any human expression? After all, that is—profoundly—why we read, and why literary critics continue to study John Milton.

There are a number of reasons why I think "queering," as these essays do it, has things to tell us, invisible seams we may not see or understand about Milton's work, as David Orvis discloses in *Doctrine and Discipline*, where the myth of Anteros functions as a figure of queer desire that belies the overt heterosexuality of Miltonic marriage. Admittedly, what I am about to say reflects my own conception of the poet, his influences and his times; but there are many Milton critics, past and present, who have seen the things I have seen in his writings. "Queering" emphasizes what Milton does, namely, the great fact of creatural life—embodiment—which deity honors with an immanent and then incarnate and always personal God. Indeed, for Milton, there can be no creatural knowledge of God or the world without embodiment, which serves as the threshold between self and other. This is not to say that, for Milton, mind and body are identical (the monist thesis), nor are they necessarily antagonistic (the dualist thesis): rather, our experience of them entails a distinction—a *seam* between these contingent and inextricable modes of creatural being, whose operations are mutual but not the same. Self is created from the bodily experience which connects it to the world, but that experience is no more its objective correlative than the body's appearances or the human conventions of identity.

Milton makes this argument in the *Second Defense*, where he says that his body makes him a liar against his will since he does not look blind, and that both conscience and experience refute the accusation that his loss of sight was God's condign punishment for writing against the king. But he was an apostle of incongruity long before his blindness, contending throughout the tracts that neither the experience of continuity nor totality belong to human being. To be a creature is to be embodied, mortal, finite, which for Milton constitutes the condition of our separateness, and of our needful sympathy with things which share the same bodily existence we do. He writes the tracts out of this awareness, as the figures of eccentricity and contiguity attest, which are equally the hallmarks of divine as well as human creativity. Incongruity is also the problem that besets his speakers from the companion poems to *Lycidas*, the sonnets, *Samson* and his two epics, who always find themselves at odds with their world. If it is true, as T.S. Eliot complains, that Milton does not feel his thought "as immediately as the odour of a rose" (Eliot 1 247); that his imagery is "all general," lacking Donne's or Shakespeare's pungent particularity (Eliot 2 140); that "the inner meaning is separated from the surface, and tends to become something occult, or at least without effect upon the reader until fully understood" (Eliot 2 143), then the reasons lie for Milton in the "seam" or distinction between these inseparable modes of human being, mind and body, which find their way into his poetry in subtle and elusive ways.

For Milton, it is an issue of idolatry at the level of poetic image and syntax, in which he would not have us absorbed in the way Eliot the Imagist desires, and first Satan and the apostate, then Eve and Adam do, to their great loss. To rest in unreflective sensation denies the distinction between mind and body, self and experience, the evident and inevident sense of things, what immediately appears and what proves in time to be the case, which constitutes an interlude of indefiniteness, uncertainty, contingency, in which assumption and expectation can be turned upside down. This is of course the temptation endured by Our Saviour, his mother and disciples in *Paradise Regained*, and the question raised by Samson's inner promptings, even to the end. And as in queer theory, the distinction introduces aesthetic issues on which critics have commented since the publication of the late poetry, but which currently have gone by the board in Milton studies. Whether the reader is for or against Milton's poetics, they can generally agree about its effects, as I can agree with Eliot's familiar comments here while placing a construction on them that instead justifies Milton's practice:

> In Milton there is always the maximal, never the minimal, alteration of ordinary language. Every distortion of construction, the foreign idiom, the use of a word in a

> foreign way or with the meaning of the foreign word from which it is derived rather than the accepted meaning in English, every idiosyncrasy is a particular act of violence which Milton has been the first to commit. There is no cliche, no poetic diction in the derogatory sense, but a perpetual sequence of original acts of lawlessness. Of all modern writers of verse, the nearest analogy seems to me to be Mallarme, a much smaller poet, though still a great one. (Eliot 2 154)

We have forgotten what John Crowe Ransom, himself a poet like Eliot, said about Milton's poetry, which he disliked: that it is deeply, deliberately experimental, which Eliot's reference to Mallarme underscores. We tend to think the so-called "metaphysical" poets experimental; but as Eliot observes, in their conceitfulness they are not only recognizably linked to Donne but obviously and often explicitly to the Tudor Petrarchanists. Milton, however, is unique in his poetics, even inimitable because his imitators reproduce the superficies but not the effect of his words. As Dr. Johnson complains, he is as idiosyncratic as one can be in the English tradition, which Johnson puts down to his republicanism and hatred of authority. I will not rehearse this aspect of the Milton controversy, which Christopher Ricks has intelligently if not definitively handled; but since queer theory is itself inclined towards an aesthetic of incongruity, I would observe that Milton's poetics share that inclination in a different if comparable fashion.

It is a peculiarly allusive and analytic idiom, whose manifold—and I have argued, ironical—meanings are shaped and disclosed precisely by their deviation from those common usages and patterns of speech which Dr. Johnson, Eliot and others approve. But regardless, it is fidelity to the actual vicissitudes of human experience, in tension with just such assumptions and expectations, that configures the embodied self and makes poetry "simple, sensuous and passionate" for Milton. As early as the Third Prolusion, he argues this very Baconian point (made in both the *Advancement* and *De Augmentis*) against scholastic logic as a medium of knowledge, for which he would substitute the "sensible and plausible" speech of poetry, rhetoric and history. Those orders of expression possess the affective power to move the whole human being, not just the intellect, to understanding, decision and action, which for a public man like Milton proposes to be, is the proper means by which "to inculcate wisdom [and] to incite to noble acts" (*YP* 1:246). By contrast, the problems of scholastic philosophy "have no existence in reality at all, but like unreal ghosts and phantoms without substance obsess minds already disordered and empty of real wisdom," contributing "neither to the general good nor to the honour and profit of our country, which is generally considered the supreme purpose of all sciences" (*YP* 1:245-46).

Moreover, as with queering, the predicament of embodiment makes his poetry, and indeed all his writings including *Christian Doctrine*, acutely personal. If anyone does, Milton writes out of his experience, his private joys and sorrows, although the lyric ego is not his own but a self that must learn what the author already knows—a process which is consistently, methodically pictured in the poetry, but never its consumation. The very sense of the word "embodied" carries the force of a distinction (but no division) between self and its corporeal being, which queering also argues against identitarian claims and Milton expresses by Eve's "unexperienced" displacement of her being onto its amorous reflection (*LM:PL* 4.457): she knows self solely as unreflective sensation and emotion, but remains ignorant of its source until the divine voice intercedes to tell her that what she admires and then adores is the body's image of itself, with speech (as it often does in myth) separating self from undifferentiated experience. From this distinction arises that curious belief with which humanity is afflicted, namely, that we are made or rendered bodily, as if we had been otherwise, only to find our selves abruptly—and sometimes falsely—incarnated here. But as Adam describes his birth, we do so because consciousness awakes to the body and the world simultaneously: it learns the body as it learns the world to which sensation inextricably connects it. And as the body changes with each sensation, so the self grasps the contingency of creaturely existence and thereby the limit conditions of human being, subject both within and without to the body's transformations.

Thus Milton pictures the contingency of this vital relation between self and body in picturing how our first parents differently come to bodily awareness; and queering also understands that not everyone experiences embodiment in the same way. Despite the enthralling immediacy of our sensations and passions, the body does not necessarily feel like self or even part of self, especially when it forces its existence upon our consciousness by its demands or frailties. At that point, it seems antipathetic, estranging. To a certain extent, Samson's crisis is not his bondage to the Philistines but his bondage to a body he no longer recognizes—now blind and inert, an alien assemblage, Dagon's mirror image, where it had once been glorious, seamless, miraculous in its strength. And without his familiar body, not to mention his hair, Samson has lost his familiar identity and relation to his God, which he fears may have been delusional all the while. He has also been displaced, not least by his enslavement, from the collective decorum of bodily being that his or any community assumes for its members, not only in appearance, movement and speech, but in the very feelings these express, as Uriel detects the presence of the fallen on earth when he spies Satan "disfigured, more than could befall / Spirit of happy sort" by his "gestures fierce" and "mad demeanor" (*LM: PL* 4.127-28).

But sympathy for the devil is wasted here since the apostate are the incontinent conformists of *Paradise Lost*, and their great chief imperializing when it comes to identity, who invents the dogma of the angels' autochthonous birth; who sees himself and his predicament reflected everywhere he looks; and whose drive for the self-identical would have everyone, including God, confined in doxological fashion to "mutual amity so strait, so close, / That I with you must dwell or you with me" (*LM: PL* 4.375-77). The problem with this plan is that deity is not as it appears to be, much to Satan's hysterical dismay, who had supposed himself to be uniquely like God, only to discover at the exaltation that he was only like God's firstborn creature and divine similitude, the Son. The weird fruit of this perceived demotion, Sin, produced out of Satan's own narcissistic brain, comes so palpably to resemble her father (or he her) that he is moved to copulate with his own image in a Miltonic satire on more than Satan's titanic narcissism. For Milton's devil is a rationalist who claims his reason notionally equalled the divine, if only by reducing deity to the sum of its palpable parts, and who "brings / a mind not to be changed by place or time" (*LM: PL* 1.253-54), declaring to himself and his followers the rationalist manifesto that "The mind is its own place, and in itself / Can make a heaven of hell, a hell of heaven" (*LM: PL* 1.252-53).

Indeed, the creaturely attempt to escape bodily existence Milton treats as pathological and regularly ascribes to Satan, whose denial of his embodied condition is made actual in a way Marlowe would recognize, when the devil laments on Mt. Niphrates, "Which way I fly is hell; myself am hell" (*LM: PL* 4.75). I refer here to Milton's persistent phenomenalism, in which the quality of one's experience depends upon the mind that receives it, as Marlowe's Faust discovers, which at the same time can be no less real for that contingency. Such is the symbiosis between body and mind. One of the reasons Satan undertakes his journey out of hell is because he thinks—until the moment when he arrives—that he can alter the condition of himself and his followers, a delusion that precipitates the Almighty's first joke ("seest thou what rage / Transports our adversary" [*LM: PL* 3.80-81]), and Satan's despair. For he cannot leave hell or change his state for the better: having rejected the source of life in his creator, he has deprived himself of the capacity to grow, learn and change, repent and convert, which attend the reasonable creature's conscious, faithful relation to God. He and the apostate have thus consigned themselves forever to the state of the living dead, condemned to endless circularity and reiteration, whether in hell or the new world, and a landscape bereft of such possibilities—where "peace / And rest can never dwell, hope never comes / That comes to all" (*LM: PL* 1.65- 67).

As everyone knows, Milton explores the predicament of his own blindness but also of his exceptionality in the figure of Samson, whose sightlessness is not only physical but spiritual; Satan in his solipsism is another such figure, as is the suffering speaker of *Paradise Lost* and of one of Milton's greatest sonnets, "When I consider how my light is spent." The conviction of being a person set apart, almost congenital to Milton's writings, is not owing to a complacent superiority or a blind faith in the manifest destiny of his cause. It is evident that, at various junctures in his life, Milton experienced the world he believed governed by a just and good God as incoherent, inordinate, unjust. Such responses are very human; but the doubt they may inspire can lead to profound shifts in understanding, to adamant disbelief on the one hand, or to theodicy on the other—the vindication of God's ways—which early became the chief problematic of Milton's art. His peculiar sense of injustice, of incoherence, appears to consist in the felt discrepancy between his reception and his sense of self, specifically, the exceptional sensations of his own genius whose sheer power and celerity the proems of *Paradise Lost* express to some extent, and with whose capacities he kept faith by a lifetime of intellectual as well as artistic travail. The affinity with Samson needs no explanation, except to insist like Donne in *Death's Duel* on the irreducible ambiguity of that biblical example.

Milton experienced this discrepancy almost from the start (and certainly from his twenty-third year, if the sonnet "How soon hath time" is any index), which undoubtedly made genius a burden as much as an afflatus. The burden was likely increased by the very eccentricity which makes his poetry strange, queer, and which appears to have been greeted with derision ("the Lady of Christ's") at Cambridge—derision to which his career as a controversialist amply exposed him. More to the point, his reception led Milton to fear that those powers of which he had the most intimate experience would prove not only unproductive, inevident, but ultimately illusory. For although he knew his genius from its sensations, it signified only a capacity, a potential, which however astonishing could remain forever inconsumate, thwarted by the consequences of his own choices—the work of his "left hand." In his biography of the poet, William Parker mentions "the troubling sense of isolation that comes in time to the gifted" (Parker 1:7), and which inflects Milton's repeated pleas for a fit audience, though few (*LM: PL* 7.31). This was no convention, nor are the autobiographical passages which dot his tracts the effusions of an overblown ego, for both of which he has been much ridiculed. They derive instead from an abiding anxiety to be known as he experienced himself, and not as he seemed, which again is a very human desire.

When the speaker of *Paradise Lost* dreads that "an age too late, or cold / Climate, or years damp my intended wing / Depressed" and so rob his "higher argument" of its due fame, he confesses a similar fear, to which he adds the further aggravation, "and much they may, if all be mine, / Not hers who brings it nightly to my ear" (*LM: PL* 9.44-47). As it always has, the figure of the muse signifies an extraordinary access of imaginative power, which Milton by then surely knew he had; but here, in the context of fame, the muse is invoked to assuage the speaker's anxiety about the reception of his art in a hostile world, with he himself "fallen on evil days, / On evil days though fallen, and evil tongues: / In darkness, and with dangers compassed round, / And solitude" (*LM: PL* 7.24-28). Those who mock Milton for the interregnum between his claims and his achievements also ignore his passionate political commitments, unless to depress them by observing that they produced the rule of Charles II, not the saints. But in reducing such expressions to an egotism resolutely oblivious to the popular failure of himself, his ideas and his cause, they betray the *schadenfreude* of those who resent genius, not having it themselves.

But if Miltonic embodiment has its perplexities, it also has its raptures. Notwithstanding the dearth of that T.S. Eliot sought and could not find there, the world of Milton's poetry is full of noises, sounds and sweet airs, voice and echoes; palpable, mutable atmospheres, winds and breezes; wafting fragrances, tastes, textures and touch; amber light and darkness visible (a paradox, not an oxymoron), as well as the access of instinct, emotion and idea these affections of the body incite in the minds which experience or imagine them. And none of this sensation is a mere backdrop to the action but methodically contributes to its distinctive qualities and significance. Moreover, heavenly beings in *Paradise Lost* are no less embodied than human ones because they are no less creatural. Thus Raphael proves to a bemused Adam—smitten by the archangel's "glorious shape" (*LM: PL* 5.309), "whose excellence he saw / Transcend his own so far" (*LM: PL* 5.456-57)—that star ladies like himself do indeed go the bathroom, which the archangel does by eating with "keen dispatch / Of real hunger and concoctive heat / To transubstantiate" his food in Milton's satirical usage. As Raphael explains, both human and angelic being have

> Within them every lower faculty
> Of sense, whereby they hear, see, smell, touch, taste,
> Tasting concoct, digest, assimilate,
> And corporeal to incorporeal turn.... (*LM: PL* 5.409-15)

For "whatever was created, needs / To be sustained and fed," in a cosmic alimentary round from earth to sea, to air and fire, moon and sun (*LM: PL* 5.415-30). Angelic sex can only be next.

Thus the spectrum of creaturely existence pictured by the archangel in Book Five—inanimate, sentient, instinctual, reasonable and intelligential—knows no sharp divisions since all are made by God, who alone is absolutely other as creator distinguished from creature, unmade from made, causeless from caused, infinite from finite: "When we speak of knowing God, it must be understood with reference to the imperfect comprehension of man; for to know God as he really is, far transcends the power of man's thought, much more of his perception [*nam Deus, prout in se est humanam cogitationem, nedum sensus longe superat*]" (*CM* 14:30-31). Milton's *Christian Doctrine* begins with two seemingly contradictory principles—God's existence and God's incomprehensibility—which work not to invalidate scripture's account of deity but paradoxically to reinforce it, as the only authentic religious knowledge available and intelligible to humanity, not least because God himself has provided it.

We are not, Milton says, to speculate about the divine nature but instead to conceive God as he "shows and describes himself in the sacred writings [*qualem in sacris literiis ipse se exhibet, seque describit*]," but with this critical proviso—that "he is not so constituted in himself, but of the sort we can grasp [*non qualis in se est, sed qualem nos capere possumus*]" (*CM* 14:30, my very literal translation). Milton deliberately refrains from using the Latin equivalents of "image," "picture," "form" or even "conception" to which Sumner and Kelley have recourse, much less their interpolated "corresponds." His preference for verbs over nouns, and his use of the indefinite phrase, *qualis . . . talem*, make the iconoclastic point that, for us, deity is never an object for us to know, only a meaning for us to grasp. Similarly, the interpolated concept of correspondence suggests that scriptural expressions permit us to make a stable, discrete and intelligible correlation between the expressions of the text, as we understand them, and the divine nature. This was of course Job's mistake, who assumed he could confine deity to the covenant's picture of the Lord; thus the creator God's theopany from the whirlwind obliges Job to confess that "I have uttered what I did not understand, / things too wonderful for me, which I did not know" (Job 42:3). That is, in our human finitude, we simply cannot say *how* deity is as scripture depicts it, only that it is so.

Thus those critics who have sought systematically, in the scholastic fashion, to organize *Christian Doctrine*'s account of the divine attributes inevitably hit an impasse, because Milton consistently refuses to say more about God than (in his view) scripture itself does, and that includes whatever it leaves unsaid about the interrelations among its images. Like the Protestant reformers, he makes our knowledge of God, whom "we must call WONDERFUL and INCOMPREHENSIBLE," effectively groundless (*YP* 6:152)—a matter of faith. So if we want to know the unknowable God, we should think of the divine as scripture speaks of it, but without supposing that its God-talk is either factual or symbolical, and thus grounds for extrapolations to the nature of religious *invisibilia*. Since no one "can form correct ideas about God guided by nature or reason alone, without the word or message of God" (*YP* 6:132), there is no curtain of phenomena that reason can boldly thrust aside to disclose the divine reality, nor can we speculatively infer the divine nature by analogy either to our own or creation's:

> For granting that, both in the literal and figurative descriptions of God, he is exhibited not as he really is, but in such a manner as may be within the scope of our comprehensions, yet we ought to entertain such a conception of him, as he, in condescending to accommodate himself to our capacities, has shown that he desires we should conceive. For it is on this very account that he has lowered himself to our level, lest in our flights above the reach of human understanding, and beyond the written word of Scripture, we should be tempted to indulge in vague cogitations and subtleties. [*Quamvis enim hoc concedatur, Deum, non qualis in se est, sed qualem nos capere possumus, talem semper vel describi vel adumbrari, nos tamen nihilo minus debebiums talem prorsus nostra concipere, qualis ipse sed captum accommodans no*strum, *vult concipi; ob id ipsum enim se ad nos demisit, ne nos elati supra captum humanum supraque quod scriptum est, vagis cogitationibus atque argutiis locum daremus.*] (*CM* 14:30-33)

The consequence of this radical constraint upon inference, which expresses the distinction between creature and creator, is that we are neither to add to or subtract from the scriptural picture of God according to our own judgments: "to do so would be to follow the example of men, who are always inventing more and more subtle theories about him" (*YP* 6:134). Thus Milton rejects the theological ascription to God of human feelings (anthropopathy) *except* as the sacred text applies such ideas to him. When scripture says of God that he "repents," "is grieved in his heart," "rested and was refreshed," "feared the enemy's displeasure," Milton exhorts the reader to ascribe these emotions to him as a *picture* devised to convey what remains perpetually beyond our understanding, and for us to use in order to have relationship with the divine: "let us believe that it is not beneath God to feel what grief he does feel, to be refreshed by what refreshes him, and to fear what he does fear" (*YP* 6:135).

Response: An Apology for Queering Milton

In justifying this tact, he go so far as to enlist the *selem elohim*, in which *God is said to have created man in his own image, after his own likeness,* Gen. i. 26, and not only his mind but also his external appearance" (*YP* 6:135): "if God habitually assign to himself the members and form of man, why should we be afraid of attributing to him what he attributes to himself, so long as what is imperfect and weakness when viewed in reference to ourselves be considered as most complete and excellent when imputed to God" (*CM* 14:35). For Milton, the *selem elohim* not only emphasizes the legitimacy of scriptural anthropomorphism, which we cannot controvert, but also the dignity of human being, including the human body, to whose order of creatural existence its creator adapts his words, and enfolds his nature in the incarnation. In short, for Milton, scripture's way of speaking shows us how, miracles having ceased, to find God *in* the world, which is neither by confining significance to the superficial or ostensible sense of things, nor by denying their embodied, circumstantial force in favor of a wholesale metaphysical translation. If I may put it this way, God is always an implication of experience, as Milton explains in the first pages of *Christian Doctrine*, within phenomena but never the same as them, owing to the insuperable distinction between creature and creator, the caused and the causeless, finite and infinite.

The revelation of God through the Son and Christ, which comprise scripture's subject, effectively model this hermeneutic for Milton. Unlike his Father (in gospel usage), the Son was created by God voluntarily, "within the bounds of time" (*YP* 6:209), "endowed with the divine nature and whom similarly, when the time was ripe, God miraculously brought forth his human nature from the Virgin Mary" (*YP* 6:211). In Milton's subordinationism, the Son is not unmade or eternal but begotten by divine decree "before the foundations of the world," and possessed of the divine nature to the extent that the Father elects to bestow it upon him. As a creature, he can be seen and heard where the Father cannot, and is thus preeminently the image of God—"*the brightness of his glory and the image of his substance*"—deity's persona and himself the agent of divine creation in time, after Hebrews 1, and finally "the only mediator between God and man" (*YP* 6:211).

In short, for Milton, the Son as creature is the embodied subject of historical theophany (as are the angels), distinguished from God by his name and relation but more profoundly by his experiential status and role. Indeed, he is all that can be known of deity in this life and in *Paradise Lost*, where the angels in their song of praise reproduce Isaiah's sight of the Lord in the temple, whom Milton more than once identifies not as deity but as the Son or an angel. And with the event of the Son's incarnation as Jesus and the Christ, deity invests godhead in the bodily life of human being no less than in creatural existence with the begetting of the Son, even as the distinction is still maintained and in fact compounded: every revelation, every manifestation of the divine within time is thus not only a picture of itself that deity elects to create, but its form is always an assemblage of modes of existence distinct from each other: creator from creature, divine from human, self from experience. Yet as Milton says of the *theanthropos*—"God-man"—the Son as the person Jesus of Nazareth, they "coalesce [*coaluere*]" in each individual to form a whole person, if one with invisible seams (*YP* 6:228; *CM* 14:228).

Queer Milton

It follows from his theology that Milton has no use for any order of transcendence that is not strictly conceptual and moral, conducted within the phenomenal bounds set by human life. Disdain for the body is disdain for the creature and its creator; and it is no small irony that satanic rationalism has as its *contrapasso* the increasing incarnation of the apostate, whose refined substance gradually grows more gross with their sin even as their original glory is obscured. At the same time, Milton rejects sheer sensory engrossment of an undifferentiated, Nietzschean kind because it collapses mind with body to the exclusion of their distinction, and thus the possibility of that inevident order of existence and meaning which belongs to *res non apparentes*—those things which do not appear as such, like the hidden God, a person's self, the significance and destiny of a life or a nation, or the sense of the text. They are consequently the subject of faith, as "the assurance of things hoped for, the conviction of things not seen" in the words of Hebrews 11:1.

Thus Milton himself "cannot praise a fugitive and a cloister'd vertue, unexercis'd & unbreath'd, that never sallies out and sees her adversary, but slinks out of the race, where that immortal garland is to be run for, not without dust and heat" (*YP* 2:515). In other words, virtue is nothing if it consists in mere negation and rigid abstinence, whose "whitenesse" in Milton's own disdainful words "is but an excrementall whitenesse," because in satanic fashion it rejects the claims of experience upon understanding—a conviction the poet held as early as the companion poems and *Comus*, where (I have argued) the Lady undergoes a rape that, however figural in its expression, gives an existential edge to Miltonic chastity, not to say Comus' version of *seizing the day*. Milton's eccentric substitution of that notional virtue for charity, and his remarks on chastity in the *Apology for Smectymnuus*, where he defends himself against charges of debauchery, have given the poet the reputation of a prig. But what Milton means by chastity is not abstinence but rather temperance—the exercise of discretion, proportion, moderation in the conduct of life—and as he and the Lady argue against Comus' libertinism, the opposite of Stoic *apatheia* or indifference. A prig would not picture sex in paradise or imagine angelic coitus, nor would he write how "half her swelling breast / Naked met his under the flowing gold / Of her loose tresses hid" (*LM: PL* 4.495-97), or imagine how the "youthful beauty" of the cherub Zephon abashes Satan, who "felt how awful goodness is, and saw / Virtue in her shape how lovely, saw, and pined / His loss" (*LM: PL* 4.845-49).

There is a moral intelligence to be gained from experience, directed by sensation and emotion, that Milton will not willingly let go. Embodiment also describes the limit conditions of our mutable, finite being and consequently of our understandings, which are confined not to sensory experience as such but to the meanings that experience implicates, indicative both of evident and inevident existences and operations. It is these Adam calls "my fill / Of knowledge, what this vessel can contain; / Beyond which was my folly to aspire" (*LM:PL* 12.558-60). In other words, the "paradise within . . . happier far" that Michael promises our first parents is not subjectivity insulated from the body's sensory pollution, or a life led in antinomian anxiety (*LM:PL* 12.587). It is rather what Montaigne, that unmatched philosopher of embodiment, pronounces against all "humours soaring to transcendency":

> It is an accomplishment, absolute and as it were God-like, to know to enjoy our being as we ought. We seek other attributes because we do not understand the use of our own; and, having no knowledge of what is within, we sally forth outside ourselves. A fine thing to get up on stilts; for even on stilts we must still walk with our legs! And upon the finest throne in the world, we are seated, still, upon our arses. (Montaigne 1268-69)

Works Cited

All my biblical quotations are taken from the Revised Standard Version.

Aristotle. *Metaphysics*. Trans., Richard Hope. Ann Arbor: U Michigan P, 1960.
Browning, Andrew, ed. *English Historical Documents: Vol. VIII 1660-1714*. London: Eyre & Spottiswoode, 1953.
Carey, John and Alastair Fowler, eds., *The Poems of John Milton*, London: Longman, 1968. (*LM*).
Eliot, T. S. *Selected Essays: 1917-1932*. New York: Harcourt, Brace, 1932. (Eliot 1)
Eliot, T. S. *On Poetry and Poets*. London: Faber and Faber, 1957. (Eliot 2)
Elton, G. R. *The Tudor Constitution*. 2nd ed. Cambridge: Cambridge UP, 1982.
Johnson, Samuel. *Lives of the Poets*. 2 vols. London: Oxford UP, 1952.
Jonson, Ben. *The Complete Poems*. Ed. George Parfitt. London: Penguin, 1988.
Miller, John. *After the Civil Wars: English Politics and Government in the Reign of Charles II*. London: Pearson Education / Longman, 2000.
Montaigne, Michel de. *The Complete Essays*. Trans. and ed., M.A. Screech. London: Penguin, 1973.
Parker, William R. *Milton: A Biography*. 2nd ed. Rev.ed., Gordon Campbell. 2 vols. Oxford: Clarendon, 1996.
Patterson, Frank A., ed. *The Student's Milton*. Rev.ed. New York: Appleton-Century-Crofts, 1933.
Patterson, Frank A., et al., eds. *The Works of John Milton*. 17 vols. New York: Columbia UP, 1931-38. (*CM*).
Wolfe, Don M. et al., eds. *The Complete Prose Works of John Milton*. 8 vols. New Haven: Yale UP, 1953-82). (*YP*)

www.ingramcontent.com/pod-product-compliance
Lightning Source LLC
Chambersburg PA
CBHW081849170426
43199CB00018B/2861